SARAH and the
NUMBER KNIGHTS

Lemon Tree Press

King Maximo and the Number Knights

Multiplicando

LMNOP and All the Letters A to Z

Working With LMNOP, A Manual For Parents & Teachers

LMNOP Alphabet Wall Cards

A Knife and a Fork and a Bottle and a Cork

Chicken in the Car and the Car Can't Go

Copyright 2019 Howard Schrager – LemonTree Press

Cover Illustration by Sarah Madsen

SARAH and the
NUMBER KNIGHTS

A Companion and Sequel to
King Maximo and the Number Knights

In Which Children Discover the Qualities of Numbers through Creative Play in Nature

by Howard Schrager

Lemon Tree Press

Acknowledgements

I cannot imagine how this book, and *King Maximo and the Number Knights* on which it is based, could have been conceived without my teaching experience in the educational model which Waldorf Education has provided. I am deeply grateful to all Waldorf teachers who paved the way for this book, and to all teachers who are working to bring learning to children in developmentally appropriate ways.

I am indebted to Michael Schneider, author of *Beginner's Guide to Constructing the Universe*, whose work provided inspiration for many of the activities in this book.

It is my hope that this book will help educators to realize that the gateway to children's minds is their imagination.

"We're not working, we're playing."

Rosemary to Sir Owen

Howard Schrager

Monterey, CA

September 2019

Introduction

"Knowledge is deep within us."-Plato

While writing a manual to accompany *King Maximo and the Number Knights*, the idea came to me to create a sequel featuring the unsung hero of the story, Sarah, who answered THE QUESTION on which the story hinges, "Which is the greatest of all the numbers?"

The indications for using the story to teach mathematical concepts through hands-on activities are found within the story itself. As such, it is a textbook in story form. It is my hope that this effort will demonstrate the efficacy of this form of teaching as a means of deepening the learning experience beyond that obtained through more traditional academic instruction

The story is set in a meadow. The lawfulness of nature mirrors the lawfulness of mathematics, and vice versa. In learning through the use of imaginative, purposeful activity something is stimulated which leads to the cultivation and development of capacities we should hope to find in a dynamic human being.

The story links the study of mathematics to the natural sciences, and provides an active grounding in geometry. Work with the Number Knights touches on areas largely overlooked in most educational circles, including visualization, discernment, spatial awareness, body geography, hand/eye coordination, and the artistic sense in general. The work is primarily experiential, and as such it is strengthening and deepening in its effect.

Finally, the story portrays children working in a spirit of cooperation, mediating competitive tendencies with more social ones. The children come to realize that each has a contribution to make to the group as a whole, and that, like the Number Knights, a group is strongest when it recognizes the unique value of each of its members.

Teaching with Sarah and the Number Knights

Sarah and the Number Knights serves as a review and a deepening of the work the children have done with *King Maximo and the Number Knights* regarding the archetypal qualities of numbers. Generally speaking, I have found that the ideal time to introduce *Sarah and the Number Knights* is at the beginning of second grade. Children at this stage retain an innate openness and sense of wonder, yet they have acquired more of the conceptual and manual skills needed to carry out the activities. Having said this, I have found that children of every age take interest in the approach to learning taken here.

Time devoted to *Sarah and the Number Knights* is time well spent, preparing the soil, setting the table for further learning experiences. The children feel enthusiastic about working in this way and enjoy this lively entree into a world of mathematical concepts, which interconnect with a wide variety of other fields. As a result, their attitude toward learning becomes both more active and more receptive—qualities found in successful students.

Some teachers, understandably, are unwilling or unable to devote the requisite time to presenting both stories separately. In such instances, one could combine the two stories. In that scenario, one may first tell the story of *King Maximo* in a relatively short period of time, to give the children the requisite background, before bringing in Sarah. Alternatively, begin each chapter of *Sarah and the Number Knights* with a more detailed retelling by Sarah of what the particular knight had told of his adventure.

I encourage teachers and parents, as much as possible, and using notes if necessary, to tell the story rather than to read it. This storytelling capacity may take a bit of time to develop, but it will certainly produce a more powerful and lasting impression. Underlining key passages and phrases can be helpful. Again, this is not a story, but rather a manual in story form.

The time between presenting each new chapter may be as long or as short as circumstances warrant. Allow sufficient time for the archetype of each number to be integrated into the children's experience. After all, it was several weeks between Sarah's encounters with her friends in the meadow. If basic materials from previous chapters like sticks, stones, hoops, string or clay are made available to the children they can deepen their experience of the numbers and make new discoveries about them.

Before you present the story, refer to "The Unmanual" in the back of the book. It is best to gain an overview, to see what is feasible for your group, and to run through the activities ahead of time. Then, as you work through the chapters, visualize and practice them again. Own them. It will make the work much more fulfilling and successful for all involved.

In the story, the children listen to each other and build upon each other's experience. They wonder, they dream, they experiment, and they create. In a sense the meadow is, at once, their laboratory and their art studio. Children of all ages have a thirst, a longing, to experience the numbers as qualities, as archetypes. Much depends on this.

SARAH AND THE NUMBER KNIGHTS

They were just ordinary children. But then again, are any children just ordinary?

For a full year now and more folk had been speaking of King Maximo's Number Knights and what had been said at The Great Feast. The children who played in the meadow nearest the castle were no exception. In fact, they were the most interested of all for their friend, Sarah, was the one who had answered King Maximo's question. One day, Sarah was on her way to her parents' cottage, when she was surrounded by her former playmates.

"Sarah, was it really you who answered THE QUESTION?" "People say so," replied

Sarah. "Well, what exactly did you say at King Maximo's feast?" Mary questioned.

"I don't really remember," Sarah answered.

"Sarah, you always remember things just as people say them," Peter responded.

"Perhaps," said Sarah, "but it was my first time serving in the Great Hall and I was terribly excited! Not that people were eating. We couldn't take our eyes off the knight who was speaking. I just couldn't imagine how any number could be greater than any other, and the words just flew out of my mouth."

"C'mon, Sarah, just tell us, what did the knights say?

Peter insisted.

"Yes, what did they say?" implored several others.

"Well, I guess I could start with Sir Owen," said Sarah, thinking back to the feast.

"Sir Owen said that whatever is greatest is One."

"But one is the smallest number," Robin blurted out.

"Yes Robin, but Sir Owen insisted that it is actually the greatest," replied Sarah.

"After all, the sky, the sun, the moon, the earth, there's only one of each. It seemed

1

as though no one had ever thought of that before. Now it seems obvious. He also said that each of us is different in many ways, yet, in so many ways we are all the same. Together we are One! When Sir Owen sat down, Joccomo jumped up. He tossed his golden ball high in the air and recited:

ONE IS THE SUN

ONE IS THE SKY

ONE IS THE WORLD

AND

ONE AM I

The children found themselves clapping, for Sarah, for Joccomo, for Sir Owen. They didn't even know.

Without realizing it the children had formed a circle around Sarah. Sarah bent over and picked up a ball that the children had been kicking around.

"Here," she said, tossing the ball to Mary. "You be #1. And Daniel, you be #2."

She continued counting to 12, tossing the ball to each in turn.

"I'll be the Sun in the Middle. I'm going to toss up the ball now and call a number. If it's your number, then run after it. The rest of you run as far from the ball as you can until you hear the catcher shout STOP. Now, the catcher must roll the ball at someone close by. If it hits her, then she gets a point against her. After each roll, everyone has to get back into the circle before I count to three. Ready? Number-r-r 4..."

They played and played, but then Sarah had to go.

Next day, they went over what Sarah had told them about Sir Owen. Andrew tossed the ball into the air and recited Joccomo's verse, ending with a bow. By the time the children had said good-bye, they all could recite Joccomo's verse, and even bowed together at the end, as they imagined he would. Each day they waited

2

for Sarah, but she didn't come. That didn't stop them. "Let's play Sun-in-the-Middle," Lark cried out. And they did, over and over.

"Let's make our circle grow like a bubble," said Mary. "Now smaller, but be careful. Keep it round."

After a while Peter suggested, "Let's move the circle in the direction of the

Great Oak." And they did.

"Now let's move it over toward the Big Boulder," said Jessica.

"Now let's do the same thing, and pass the ball around the circle at the same time," suggested Daniel. So off they went. As they were doing this, a knight rode up, bringing his horse to a halt. His shield displayed a brilliant yellow sun on a blue background. The children stopped what they were doing and ran over and looked up at him.

 "We're not working, we're playing," called Rosemary, merrily.

The knight laughed heartily.

"The circle is the shape of Oneness, isn't it. All that is greatest is

One."

"Oh yes, we know," they cried. "Sarah told us everything."

"Sarah?" asked the knight.

"Yes, Sarah," Robin cried out, "the one who answered THE QUESTION!"

The knight looked thoughtful for a moment, and then he smiled, "Oh yes, Sarah."

"Boys and girls, I want to show you something. Let's go to that bare patch over

there."

All of a sudden Rosemary blurted out, "You're Sir Owen, aren't you?"

"Why, yes, I am," the knight replied.

"It's Sir Owen!" Rosemary shouted, jumping up and down.

All the children gathered around the knight.

Sir Owen took out two rings and connected them with a string. Then he picked up his staff and placed it into one of the rings, holding the staff upright.

"Now watch. I'm going to hold this still. And you," he said pointing to Andrew, "put this stick through the other ring and stretch the string. Keep it taut, now. That's it. Now walk around my staff, and keep the point of the stick in the dirt."

"There," he said, when Andrew had finished, "what do we have?"

"A circle," they cried out as one.

"Yes, a perfect circle. Now keep practicing, and keep your circles round," said the knight as he mounted his horse. The children's eyes followed Sir Owen as he rode off.

And did the children practice. There was something inside them that wanted to make the circles as round as possible. It was fun to find the exact center, too.

Hugh stood still and slowly turned around in place, holding the stick exactly still with his arm stretched out.

"I'm not looking at the line," said Anne, I'm imagining that I'm cutting out the crust for a pie."

"I just can't get the picture on Sir Owen's shield out of my mind," Jessica said. "I'm going to draw it."

"So am I" everyone seemed to say at once.

"Yours looks just like Sir Owen's," said Mary. "Somehow mine doesn't. How did you do it?"

"Well, I started by making a mark, top, bottom, left, right. Then I put two evenly spaced marks in each section."

Knowing this seemed to make everyone's circle look better, this and practice. Sir Owen had left the rings and the string. Next day, they used it to make a really big circle in the bare spot. They called it the 'Great Circle'.

It had been two weeks since Sarah had come home from the castle, and the children watched for her each day. They played Sun in the Middle, and practiced making circles in the dirt within the Great Circle. They had also begun collecting round things, apples, plums, pumpkins, and round stones from the stream. Andrew arrived one day rolling a barrel hoop with a short stick. Another day, Hugh arrived, molding clay from the stream bank into a ball. Anne brought some dough her mother had spared for her. They began to call the game, 'Bring-a-Thing'.

Mary was singing.

"What are you singing," Rosemary asked Mary. "Are you singing Sir Owen's poem?"

"Yes, Sir Owen's poem grew wings," was her reply.

TWO

It was late in the day and Sarah was trudging home from the castle, lost in thought, when the children spied her from a distance. They were hiding behind bushes when Rosemary, the youngest of them, could stand it no longer and cried out, "Sarah, where have you been?" Sarah was startled at first, but, as she was encircled by her friends, she smiled and answered, "I've had to work very hard at the castle. I've had no time for play."

"Wanna play?" called Peter. "Here," he said, tossing her an apple. She tossed it back to him as he walked backwards keeping his eyes on her. Sarah, meanwhile, was thinking, "This is not just an apple, this is a 'sphere'; that's what Sir Owen would call it. I like that word."

So, back and forth it went until the other children were doing the same with other things. Some began reciting, " One-Two, buckle my shoe, Three-Four, shut the door..."

"Now this reminds me of Sir Twain!" exclaimed Sarah. "Sir

Twain? What did he say?" asked Mary. "What did Sir Twain

say?"

"He said that two is the greatest number, because everything has its opposite: Day and Night, Left and Right, In and Out."
"Whisper and Shout," called Robin, skipping in a circle.
"Yes and No, here we go," added Elizabeth.
"Hey, how's this?" said Hugh, who was the son of a woodcutter: To and fro/The saw does go. I'm thinking of a new kind of saw that my father showed me. Two people have to work together to use it, but when they do, they can saw a huge log in two much easier than any other way. Here's how they do it," he said, showing them how two people could hold each other's thumbs and imitate sawing back and forth.
The children, of course, had to try this.

"You know," said Sarah, "Sir Twain tried to show that two is clearly seen in our bodies. Our nose has two nostrils; we have two hands, two feet, two eyes, and two ears. But," she said after pausing, "the two actually work together to do one thing, don't they, just like two knitting needles make one p i e c e o f c l o t h , or our top and bottom teeth work together to chew food. For that matter, our legs work together when we walk, and our eyes see together, if you know what I mean. I've been thinking about it a lot."

"Look," said Nick, his eyes growing wide. He was pointing to the darkening sky, suddenly turned orange and purple. The small band became quiet as they watched the glowing colors.

"The orange makes the purple look better; or does the purple makes the orange look better," wondered Daniel.

"Yes, and together they make everything look wonderful," said Rosemary, gaily.

Sarah found herself whispering,

TWO ARE MY EYES,

EARS, HANDS, AND FEET

DARK AND LIGHT

AT SUNSET MEET.

"Come on, everyone," she called, taking Rosemary's hand, "we need to get home before dark!"

Together they ran down the road toward the sun setting beyond the town.

Next day they were back in the meadow.
"Listen to this," called Robin, "Up and down/Sky and ground."

"That's good," responded Anne. "I have one, too. It goes 'Night and day/Work and play'."

"That's really good, too!" said Lark.

"How's this? Happy and sad/Good and bad," said Mary.

"Here's mine," said Peter, "Hill and valley/Street and alley."

"Win or lose/Pick and choose," said Daniel.

"I and you/You and I/Crust and filling make a pie," said Lark, proudly.

"Now that takes the cake!" cried Jessica.

"What about Bring-a-Thing?" asked Hugh, who was getting dizzy from all the rhymes.

"I brought this coin," said Daniel.

"How's that 'two'?" Hugh questioned.

"Well, the coin has two sides."

"Oh," said Hugh," "I get it. Well, my mother says there are two sides to every story. That's almost the same thing, isn't it?"

The children hadn't forgotten about their circle, or about Sir Owen. They wanted to 'keep it in shape', they said. In fact, they had gotten so good that they could keep the circle turning while they moved it around the meadow.

They were concentrating so hard that they were not aware that someone had ridden up. "Hold it there" the knight shouted, jumping down from the saddle.

"I can't believe my eyes! Now just move your circle a little closer to the one on the ground. That's it. Perfect! Now you, young fellow, come here," he said, pointing to Nick. "What do you see?"

"Well, I guess I see two circles the same size," said Nick uncertainly. "And one circle is taking a bite out of the other."

"And what do you see?" Sir Twain asked Mary.

"I see that each circle is taking a bite out of the other, too."

"Yes, it does look that way, said the knight.

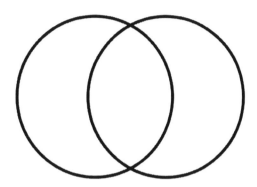

"And what do you see?" he asked, beckoning to Daniel.

"Strange as it seems, it looks like there's an almond in the middle," said Daniel.

Some children laughed, which made Daniel feel uncomfortable.

"Children, don't be so quick to laugh. It often looks like an almond to me, too. Listen, though, I was on an errand, when what you were doing caught my eye. I must take my leave now."

The children were sad to see Sir Twain going and they were quiet for some time.

"Sir Twain's shield was quite simple, wasn't it," said Elizabeth, at last. "Red over green on a slant."

"I wonder why he divided his shield the way he did?" mused Daniel. "He could have split it in the middle, side by side, or above and below."

"I like the way he did it," stated Nick. "There's something about the slanted line."

Before they left that day, Nick drew Sir Twain's shield in the Great Circle.

In the morning there were green leaves on one part and bright red petals on the other. No one knew who'd done it.

As soon as the children saw it, they began drawing other shields, filling in both sides with stones, acorns, petals, leaves and other things.

Next day the leaves were back, but matched with a different color.

Andrew picked up the hoop and laid it on the ground, twisting it back and forth until he had etched a circle in the dirt. Then he laid the hoop back on the ground, taking the exact right-sized bite out of the first. One day they made the overlap in the center a third color.

With practice several of the children were able to draw the two overlapping circles with a stick. Others used the hoops. For days they found themselves doodling in the dirt.

"Look at this!" cried Jessica. "I connected the centers of the two circles with a line. They share the line. I like that."

"And look at this," said Nick, connecting the places where the circles crossed, "the top to bottom line cuts it perfectly in half."

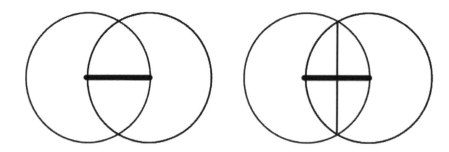

THREE

The children were growing impatient. If they were going to meet up with Sarah, they were going to have to waylay her again. They had gotten up before dawn and were waiting for her when she walked by on her way back to the castle. This time she didn't smile when they surrounded her.

"I'm in a hurry," she said.

"Please, Sarah," begged Elizabeth, "just tell us something about the next Number Knight. We can't wait any longer."

Sarah slowed her pace, but kept walking.

"All right then, the Three Bears, a three-legged stool, and these," she said at last, picking up three sticks and thrusting them toward Elizabeth. "Triangles, three sides and three angles, that's what Sir Thrice spoke about. It's as simple as one, two, three." With that, she quickened her pace. The children did not follow.

Before long, they'd all picked up sticks, which the last week's storm had provided.

"Now let's see," said Andrew, not one to turn down a challenge, "if a triangle has three sides, then it also has three corners, see."

"Not corners," said Lark, who was also fitting her sticks together, "Sarah said they were called 'angles'."

"Alright, angles," replied Andrew. "Same thing."

"What's so special about triangles, anyway?" asked

Nick.

"Isn't that what we're trying to find out? Isn't that the challenge Sarah gave us?" said Mary.

The children were all busy fitting the sticks together. "Look at all the different triangles we have," Rosemary exclaimed.

"Yes," agreed Mary, "the only thing that's the same is that they all have three sides and three angles."

"They kind of look like little sheep pens," said Nick. "I wonder why they don't make the pens this shape?"

"I'll tell you why," answered Lark, putting some pebbles inside, "the sheep would get stuck in the corners."

"What good are triangles then, anyway?" thought Nick as they walked home.

One day, Elizabeth brought a big ball of string.

"Look what my mother gave me for Bring-a-Thing," she called to Mary.

"Here, catch."

"Got it," said Mary.

Robin, ever the mischievous one, took the middle of the string and pulled on it.

"Stop it, you scamp," cried Elizabeth.

"No, wait," said Mary, "look at what he's done, he's almost made a triangle. I'll just toss the ball back to you."

Robin, meanwhile, kept moving around while holding the string with one finger. Each time he moved, a different triangle was formed.

"I have an idea," announced Peter. "Let's have each of us stand at one point on the Great Circle. Then we can toss the string to three points, and see what kind of triangles we come up with."

"Elizabeth, you be at the top," said Mary. "After all, you brought the string."

All agreed, with each finding a place on the Great Circle.

A variety of triangles appeared, and the children noticed many things. On most of them they noticed that the sides were of different lengths.

"This one looks like two legs walking," said Daniel. "Two of the sides are the same length. And I would bet that two of the angles are the same, too."

"One thing I've noticed," stated Nick, "is that when one angle is small, it gives the others a chance to be bigger."

"I think you have something there," agreed Mary. "And vice-versa. When one angle is small, the others are bigger," she added.

The game went on for quite a while with children noticing different things. After they'd made one particular triangle, Mary said, "There's something special about this triangle, and I think I know what it is. All the sides are the same, and all the angles too."

"Yes, it is really the most perfect triangle," offered Anne, "beautiful even."

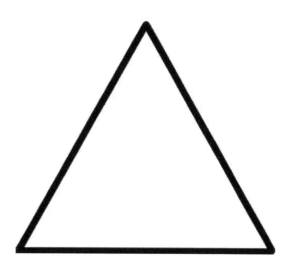

The children were fascinated by the 'Beautiful Triangle', as they'd come to call it. Jessica went to the top of the circle and walked to the three points that had made the Beautiful Triangle.

"It's easy," she said, "because they're four spaces apart." After she had done this a few times, the others could see the pattern, and they wanted to try too. It was as if they could feel it in their bones.

Before long they had walked to the three points so much that they had worn a triangular path in the dirt. Rosemary decided to count her steps. "One, two, three, four, FIVE; six, seven, eight, nine, TEN; eleven, twelve, thirteen, fourteen, FIFTEEN."

"Now," said Andrew, "I'm going to do it by threes. After all there are three sides to a triangle." Leaping, he counted, "One, two THREE, four, five SIX, seven, eight, NINE." Each time, he got to the angle exactly as he finished his third leap.

Before long, they had all taken up the challenge and were trying to get "around" the triangle with different numbers of steps.

The next day they found that they could make triangles anywhere, just by walking the shape. So long as the steps were the same size, and the angle was right, they would form the Beautiful Triangle.

Finally, Andrew etched it into the Great Circle with a stick.

Anne was braiding Mary's hair.

"It takes three sections of hair to make a braid," A n n e said. "It's so obvious, but I hadn't noticed before. Just thinking about the numbers makes me notice things."

"We've completely forgotten about Bring-a-Thing," Nick said suddenly.

"I haven't!" said Rosemary, producing a trillium flower from her hair.

" I haven't either," said Hugh. "It was just too heavy to bring. I've been stacking the biggest logs my father has cut."

He laid two on the bottom and then one on top.
"Like this," he said, taking two round stones and putting a third on top. He observed for a moment and hen he took off the top stone and laid it on the ground above the other two.

"These are both triangles, he said with certainty.

"I didn't forget, either," said Nick. "I noticed that the finest houses in the village have triangles in their roofs. I couldn't bring the houses, but I think you know what I mean," he said, drawing in the dirt.

"And I was talking with my father about triangles," said Peter. "As you know he's a mason. He said that the archways in the town wall, and also in the church, are triangles, though somewhat curved."

"And look what we're standing on every day," said Elizabeth, plucking a three-leafed clover. "It even has the shape of number 3 in it. See, around the edge?"

"Yes, that's right," noted Mary.

"The three-legged stool!" exclaimed Jessica. "I'm thinking of the stool that Sarah had mentioned! Three makes thing stand firmly. Even if the ground is bumpy, the stool doesn't wobble."

"Didn't Sarah also mention the Three Bears?" Lark questioned.

"What did she mean by that?"

"Well, let's see," said Mary. "There was Papa Bear, Mama Bear, and Baby Bear? And there was a big bowl, a middle-sized bowl, and a small bowl. And the porridge was either too hot, too cold, or just right."

"And," Robin added, "there were three chairs— a high one, a middle-sized one, and a low one. As for the beds, one was hard, one soft, and one just right."

"And, like all stories, it has a beginning, a middle, and an end. Like so many things, come to think of it," said Anne.

"There's yesterday, today, and tomorrow," Peter offered, to a discussion that was becoming quite exciting.

"Good, better, best," said Mary.

"Easy, easier and easiest," said Peter, smiling at their discoveries.

"Late, later, latest possible time to get home before dark. Let's get going," said

Jessica.

The children all headed home for the night, but they couldn't wait to get back to the meadow. Each day seemed to add more discoveries.

"You're not going to believe what I discovered," said Nick proudly. "I was drawing the overlapping circles yesterday and just doodling, when I started connecting things the way I like to do. I drew a line from the top where the circles cross, right through the center of both of the two circles, like this.

It seemed unfinished, so I drew one more line, like this."

"The Beautiful Triangle," the children gasped.

One day, just as the children were tossing the string in the form of the Beautiful Triangle, a knight rode up.

 "I see you are working with triangles," he said, taking in the scene.
"Yes, Sarah has told us about what Sir Thrice said on the night of the feast," said Elizabeth proudly.

"Oh, Sarah!" the knight replied, smiling. "I've heard a lot about her, and about you children, too. Both Sir Owen and Sir Twain have spoken of their encounters."

"Are you Sir Thrice, by any chance?" Mary asked.

"Why, yes I am, as you can see," he said, holding his shield aloft.

"Now, allow me," he said, stepping over to the Beautiful Triangle etched in the dirt. "Tell me when my sword hovers over the middle of this side, alright."

"There," the children chorused.

"Exactly," said Sir Thrice, making a mark.

"Now for this side," he said, moving his sword. Again, they were right on the mark.

"And for the third…"

"There!" the children called out excitedly.

"Good. Now watch," said the knight as he connected the three points.

Sir Thrice had just drawn the last line when Robin started jumping up and down. "The Beautiful Triangle, the Beautiful Triangle, the Beautiful Triangle is now four Beautiful Triangles, all in one!" he exclaimed.

"Hooray for Sir Thrice," the children shouted.

"Thank you, children. I must be on my way now. I'm off to pay a visit to Thomas the Tinker."

"Thomas the Tinker!" cried Elizabeth. "He's my father."

"Really!" exclaimed the knight as he mounted his horse. "Well, I'll be. I will certainly tell him I met you. So long, children," he called to them as he galloped away.

Next day Andrew challenged himself to lash together a Beautiful Triangle. Before long there was a small stack of them, all the same size. He laid one down and looked at it thoughtfully. Then he carefully laid another one on each side.

"The Four-in-One Triangle!" the children cheered.

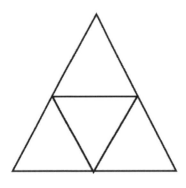

FOUR

"Sarah, can you come out and play with us. We know you're in there," called Jessica boldly.

"But it's my first day off in a month," Sarah called back, poking her head out the door of her parents' cottage.

"How about later?" Jessica pleaded.

"Oh, all right, I'll meet you in the meadow." Sarah missed her friends, and missed playing, but she did enjoy working at the castle, despite the hard work. There were so many interesting people coming and going. And the Number Knights were still there, all except Sir Pentagonal, of course, who couldn't wait to get back to the Castle of the First Rose.

The children saw Sarah coming, and rushed to meet her.

"Sarah, is it true that Sir Foursquare acts just like a bull?" Lark asked, urgently.

"Well," answered Sarah, "he is very strong, and a bit gruff, but he really is quite nice."

"What did he say about four?" demanded Nick. "That's what I want to know."

"Tables and chairs, tables and chairs," bellowed Sarah, imitating Sir Foursquare.

"Whatever does that mean?" asked Mary.

"He said that four makes things strong," said Sarah clearly. "He said that wherever he went he saw people working with four-sided things. Tables and chairs that furniture makers make are square, and they have four legs. Walls and ceilings and floors are square, too. Weaving looms are basically square, and farmers' fields are usually square. And there's more. There are four main directions- north, south, east and west. Not to mention the four-legged animals, the cow, for instance, that stands squarely on the earth throughout the four seasons- summer, fall, winter and spring." Sarah took a deep breath and went on.

"It's the same with bread," he said. We start with flour from earth grain, and then add water. Air allows the dough to rise, and then, of course, it is baked it in the fiery oven."

Just hearing all of this made the children want to do something themselves, so they set about collecting sticks, and putting them together.

"Somehow, when you build something it just seems to want to become square," said Peter looking up.

The children had made imaginary sheep pens out of the sticks that were lying around.

"Sheep pens seem to be square, but they're not always so," observed Anne. "They're only square-ish. The corners are square. The sides aren't always the same length, though."

"This one is square," called Peter. "All the sides are the same length."

"And the corners too," added Rosemary. "

"The angles," reminded Elizabeth, looking to Sarah. "All

right, the angles," Rosemary said grudgingly.

"Yes, but this one isn't a square," said Mary. "Only the sides opposite each other are the same. There are two short sides and two long sides."

"That's a rectangle," said Sarah. "That's what the Number Knights call it."

It seemed that at least once a day the ball of string came out.

"Let's see what we can do with four," said Mary.

Everyone took a place on the Great Circle. "Here's one," Elizabeth called as she tossed the ball of string to Andrew.

"And here's two," said Andrew tossing it to Rosemary.
"Three," said Rosemary, tossing it to Lark.

"And this is four," said Lark, getting it back to Elizabeth.

"It is four-sided," said Mary, "but it isn't square. What shall we do?"

"Let's see," said Peter, who was trying hard to figure out the problem, "a square has four sides that are the same length, right. How can we skip the same number of places in our circle of twelve?"

"Well," said Mary, "it can't be two places. That would not do. How about three? Three, six, nine, twelve. I think that's it. Let's see."

The children quickly got into their places on the Great Circle.

"Okay, let's go," said Mary.

Together they counted, "One, two, THREE; four, five, SIX; seven, eight, NINE; ten, eleven, TWELVE."

"We did it!" chorused the children.

Soon they had seen that they could start at any spot on the circle, and it would turn out square, if they counted by three. Still, they liked it best starting at the top. Before long there was a square within the circle. And once again, Andrew just had to etch it with a stick.

Lashing triangles together out of sticks had become quite a craze. Many of the children had mastered it. Now it was the time to try lashing squares. Before long there were squares everywhere.

"Let's see what doodling can do with squares," called Elizabeth. "It was so much fun with the triangles."

"Yes!" they chorused.

"Just one line at first," called Elizabeth.

There was only so much they could do with a square, or so it seemed. Most either made a line from top to bottom, or from left to right, usually in the middle of the square. Others drew it from corner to corner on a slant.

"Now two lines," called Lark.

Most either drew it this way,

or this way.

"Look at this, if you look carefully, you can even see the four itself in the square!" said Mary, retracing three of the lines.

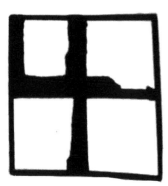

Next day they were at it again. "Look what I did! I made both crosses in the same square," called Nick.

The children rushed over to Nick to see what he had done.

In no time everyone was making this form.
After a while Jessica let out a whoop.
"Look at this!" she cried. "I had a feeling that there was another square waiting inside. I just connected the points at the four directions."

Then, without thinking, Andrew picked up a stick and started drawing on Jessica's figure.

"Look!" he cried, "This could just go on, and on, and on. I just find the middle of each side, make a mark, and then connect the marks, the same way Sir Thrice did with the triangle."

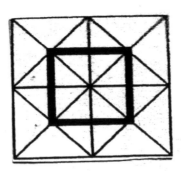

As patiently as they could, Andrew and Jessica, with help from Mary and Daniel, showed the others how it was done.

"That's not hard at all," said Hugh, after a while. "It just makes sense."

"Once you get it," added Anne.

Next day, as they were drawing in the Great Circle, the children looked up to see a horse galloping towards them. The children could see the top of a shield, but the rider was nowhere to be seen. Then they heard a thud, and suddenly the rider was standing right before them. There was no doubt that it was Sir Foursquare.

"Good day, children," he bellowed.

The children jumped back.

"Do you see this?" he asked, pounding the end of his staff into the dirt.

"This is the Staff of Uprightness. See how it stands perfectly straight on the ground, just like me, straight and tall."

'Tall', the children were thinking. They would have laughed if they had dared. Yet, when they really looked, some of them realized that even though he was short in stature, Sir Foursquare was in fact standing tall.

"I challenge someone to move my staff," the knight said gruffly.

Andrew stepped forward boldly and pulled on the middle of the staff. It didn't budge. Then he tried the bottom; still no luck. He stepped back, disappointed. Others followed, but they already knew that if Andrew couldn't do it, they would have a hard time.

"Now try," he said, tilting the staff and gesturing to Andrew. Sure enough, this time Andrew was able to move the staff.

"This, children, is the Right Angle of Sir Foursquare. It is very strong, so long as it stays straight up and down, making a square angle with the ground. After all, what is a chair with a bent leg, or a tilted chimney, or a leaning garden wall?"

"My father makes sure things are square when he is building houses," said Nick. "He even uses a tool called a square, just to make sure."

"And my father has a line with a weight that hangs straight down when he is building walls," added Peter, "to make sure everything is straight."

"That's right," said Sir Foursquare, stamping his foot.

"Now, keep up the good work, boys and girls," he said, leaping into the saddle. In a wink, he was gone.

"What about Sir Foursquare's shield?" asked Daniel. "I saw that there was a cross that divided it into four sections."

"Yes," said Mary. "I'm certain that one stood for earth, another for water, another for air, and another for fire."

Each day there were new discoveries. One day, after Jessica had drawn the first slanted line in her square, she stopped short. "How could it have taken me so long to see this?

"Right inside the square, there are two triangles."

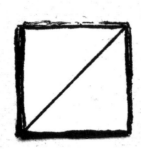

"And now, when I make the other line, there are four."

Andrew came running over to see.

"Yes," he said, "and they still have Sir Foursquare's angle, every one of them. In the middle of the cross."

Then, without thinking, he took the stick and drew a cross, up to down, left to right. "Now look at all the triangles," he said, "they still have Sir Foursquare's angles."

"There are eight, aren't there," Daniel ventured to say.

"Right," said Mary.

"We've almost lost our square to triangles," said Andrew, picking up a stick. "I've got a feeling."

With that he started connecting points.
"Now, we've got our square back. And we've got the triangles too. How many are there, anyway?"

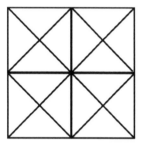

Hugh was busy counting, but Elizabeth beat him to it.
"Sixteen," she said, with assurance.
"How did you get it so fast?" asked Hugh. "I only got to four."

"Well, I saw four squares, and in each square there were four triangles. I just knew there were sixteen," said Elizabeth.

Meanwhile, the stick squares were piling up.

A few days later, Hugh came walking up fashioning a ball of clay, the same way he had done ever since the time of Sir Owen. This day, though, something was different. Maybe it was the game of dice he had been playing the night before, but today he was pressing this way and that, flattening the roundedness of the ball.
"Why Hugh, you've made a cube, just like the salt cube out in the pasture," said Lark.

"I guess I have," said Hugh, surprised at what he had done. Then he set it out for all to see.

"Why, it's just full of squares! Look at them!" cried Rosemary.

That night Nick had a dream. In it he saw one square with another square laid next to each of its sides. Then he saw the outer squares lift up on edge. In the morning, he still remembered his dream and ran to the meadow excitedly. Andrew was already there.

"Can you help me with this?" Nick asked, explaining his dream.

"Sure," said Andrew, sensing an adventure. The two started fitting the squares together, and before long, they were done, or nearly so.

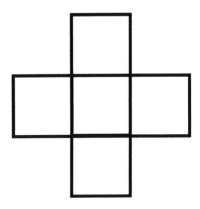

"Don't we need one more square for the top?" said Nick.

"Yes," said Andrew. "Then all we'll need is some string to hold it all together."

SIR THRICE AND SIR FOURSQUARE GO RIDING

Ever since Sir Hexagonal had spilled amethyst crystals onto the table as gifts at the Great Feast, Sir Thrice had been considering what gift he could give to the other knights. When he had ridden off to visit Thomas the Tinker, he was following through on his plan. He had shown Thomas the Four-in-One Triangle. Then it was simply a matter of Thomas folding up the tin on all three sides, and then sealing it on the top with a drop of lead.

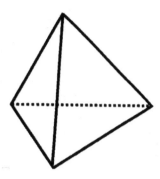

At the castle all of the knights had thanked Sir Thrice heartily for his gift, all but Sir Foursquare, that is.

"This is four-sided," he had grumbled.

Sir Thrice, knowing his friend well, at first remained silent. Then he said, "There is truth in that, my friend, therefore I suggest we put it to the test of the children."
"Good idea," agreed Sir Foursquare, "children know what's fair and square."
So off they rode.
The children listened carefully as Sir Foursquare and Sir Thrice told their stories.

Mary was the first to speak. "The way I see it is that, although there are indeed four sides, this shape is about the Four-in-One Triangle. It's just folded up."

The other children nodded, showing they agreed with Mary.

"I will not agree to this," said Sir Foursquare, storming off. In his rage, he kicked something lying on the ground. It was a large, clay cube that all the children had shaped together from river clay. Hopping on one foot, Sir Foursquare looked at the block at his feet.

"Aha!" he shouted, "every side is a square. This cube is mine! What better way to be remembered."

"But Sir Foursquare," said little Rosemary softly, "there are six sides to the cube. You can even see it on the dice we play with."

"Hmpff," was all Sir Foursquare could manage to say.

After Sir Foursquare had cooled down, Sir Thrice put his hand on his shoulder.

"My friend," he said, "look at what these children have shown us. Here's your square, but within it are many triangles, most with your special angle. And what of Sir Hexagonal, would he begrudge you the cube because it has six sides? No, we need each other. It is just as Sarah said."

FIVE

Sarah was in a good mood. She had been given the day off from work. Word had reached King Maximo that she was teaching her friends about the Number Knights. He was happy to hear that learning was spreading throughout his kingdom. The king had sent along a basket of his best apples as a token of his appreciation. Sarah passed the basket around.

"How many of you have ever seen this?" she asked, holding up the apple she had just finished cutting *the other way*.

"What?" several children questioned.

"This star," she said, "when you cut the apple this way, you can see a star."
By now the children had begun to understand. "Why have I not noticed this before?" asked Mary, thoughtfully.

"I guess we just get used to doing things the same way," added Nick.

"Well, look what happens when you break a habit," said Lark.

"That's just what happened with Sir Pentagonal," Sarah said. "Once he had seen the star hidden in the apple, he started to see it everywhere, with the help of the man with the snow-white beard, that is."

"The man with the snow-white beard?" inquired Robin.

"Yes, the man from his dream, who showed Sir Pentagonal the many things in nature which reveal a star. Just look in the flowers, the fruit, and even in us," she said, suddenly springing up into a spread-eagle stance.

"Look at me, I'm a star."

Bring-a-Thing had never been so exciting. Things they had taken for granted suddenly revealed their star forms.

"Look at all the flowers that have the star in them!" exclaimed Robin, gazing at the array of flowers within the Great Circle. "It's amazing!"

Yes, there were pansies, violets, borage, periwinkle, columbine, geraniums, buttercups, and wild roses, just to name a few. Many of them they had found right there in the meadow, or down beside the stream.

"Yeah," agreed Nick, "fruit too. I discovered it not only in our apples, but also in our pears. There's a star on the bottom."

"Yes, said Elizabeth, "and I saw it on the blueberries I was picking, but I forgot to save any. They were so tasty."

"The String Thing!" cried Andrew, suddenly.

Everyone scrambled to take their places on the Great Circle.

Without thinking, Elizabeth counted five and tossed the string to Peter. With all their practice it didn't take much to go by fives.

"Wait," cried Elizabeth, "this isn't working out as I thought it would."

"I know," agreed Mary, "it just seems to keep going. Let's follow it and see where it goes."

All agreed, and the string crisscrossed the circle many times. Just when it seemed it would never end, the string returned to Elizabeth.

"Look," she cried, "we got a star, but not the one we were looking for."

The children raised the star over their heads and looked at it from below, then they each laid their point down onto the Great Circle. They were full of amazement, but at the same time a little disappointed. While Elizabeth wound the string onto the ball, the others were trying to figure out how to make the five-pointed star within the circle. Daniel had been thinking really hard. Finally, he said, "Everything doesn't have to fit into twelve exactly, does it?"

That really got the others thinking.

"You know, said Anne, "when Sarah jumped up I imagined her within a circle, and she fit perfectly."

"Let's try doodling it," suggested Nick. "Why is this so much fun?" asked Rosemary.

"I love the way the line jumps around the circle as it forms the star," Lark remarked.

They drew hurriedly, and it wasn't long before several had made quite lovely stars.

"Yours is the best, Jessica," Anne said admiringly.

The others crowded around.

"Yes, that's certain," said Nick. "Every line is the same length, that's why."

"And look here," said Mary, excitedly. "Look at this odd form in the middle. Odd as it is, every side is the same."

"That's because every line in the star is just perfect," said Sarah knowingly.

"Sir Pentagonal loves this form."

Naturally everyone looked at the other stars. They could see that the more carefully a star had been drawn, the more beautiful the form in the middle.

As the days went on, the children found themselves walking the form of the star.

"Now how does that go, Mary?" asked Nick.

"Well look, I'll show you. Stand like Sarah did. Daniel, you hold the string up by Nick's head." Then she took the string and led it from his head to his foot, to the opposite arm, across to the other arm, down to the other foot, and back to his head.

"There it is!" said Mary.

For days the children had fun walking the star.

One day, Daniel arrived early. In the quiet morning light, he began drawing on his star, which was still etched in the dirt.

"The rooster's crowing cock-a-doodle-do, and now I'm doodling too," he said, amused by his own words.

By now doodling was second nature to all the children.

"Look what I've done," he said, joyfully! "I've made the shape from the inside on the outside, only now it's right side up."

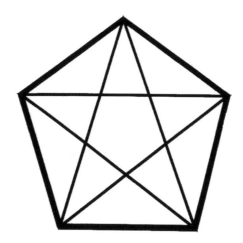

As they arrived, the children each tried this for themselves.

They were fully expecting Sir Pentagonal to appear any day, but he didn't.

Sarah, though, did return.

"I see you've made the pentagon form in quite a few ways," she said.

"Yes we have," they said proudly.

"We were expecting Sir Pentagonal, though," said Peter at last.

"You won't be seeing him for some time. Didn't I tell you, he went off to the Castle of the First Rose. Now that is a story!"

SIX

Days off became even more rare for Sarah. More and more people were coming to the castle to meet the Number Knights. Sarah didn't even seem to mind, she was learning so much. One day, Nick was playing with the stack of stick triangles, when he noticed two triangles, one atop the other. One was pointing up, and the other down.

"Look at this!" cried Nick, running to the Great Circle and laying it down. "A star with six points."

Of course, everyone soon was making one.

Suddenly, Elizabeth called out, "The String Thing," and ran to the top of the Great Circle.

Without hesitating the others hurried to their places.

"What shall we do?" asked Rosemary.

"It looks like we need two Beautiful Triangles," said Daniel. " We've made the first already, the one that points up. The other is pointing down to the bottom, so I figure the point of the second triangle has to be on #6."

"How can we get there, though?" asked Peter.

 "We just start with a new piece of string," said Mary. "Only, who gets it next?"

Several children looked at Lark in place #10.

"That's it," called out Elizabeth.

"Toss it to Lark, Hugh. It's four spaces."

"All right," said Hugh, and he threw it to Lark.

"Now send it over here," called out Jessica on place #2.

"We did it!" they cried, as the string returned to Hugh.

It wasn't long before the six-pointed star was etched in the Great Circle.
First thing, when the children arrived the next morning, they found that Anne had
etched a line connecting the six points of the star.
"I like the way the line jumps two places to make the frame," she said.
"Look in the center, said Mary. "There's the same frame form that's on the inside,
only turned a bit."

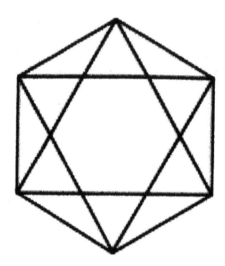

"Yes, there it is. I didn't see it right away, but we would have seen it before long,"
said Elizabeth. "It's right there before our eyes."

"We can even make the frame without making the star, All we need to do is to connect the even numbered places, like this," said Lark, drawing with a stick.

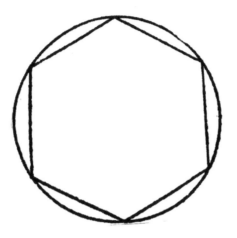

"And, look at this," said Jessica. "Here's a different kind of star. Just connect the opposite angles and you have it."

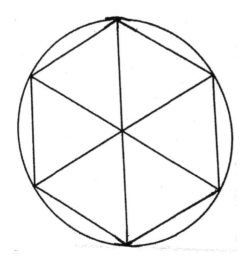

"It makes me think of a wagon wheel," said Daniel.

"Well then," said Peter, "let's try rolling it, or maybe we could move it the way we did with the circle."

While they were trying, Sarah arrived.

"Well, well," she said merrily, "it looks like Sir Hexagonal got here before me."

"No," said Mary, "none of the Number Knights has been here. We did this on our own."

The children nodded.

"How did you do it?" Sarah asked, surprised.

"It's mostly Sir Thrice, I guess. Twice thrice, that is," said Daniel, chuckling.

"Sarah, what did Sir Hexagonal say at the feast? We almost forgot to ask," said Peter.

"What did he say? Well, he told of being led by a bee."

"A bee?" said Anne, a bit puzzled.

"Yes," answered Sarah, "he was led by a bee to the hive. And on the way, the bee visited many different flowers with six petals. A lot of these grow right around here."

The children didn't need more prompting. The next morning, the Great Circle was strewn with lilies, daffodils, and hyacinths.

"Look!" marveled Rosemary. "So many lovely flowers!"

Hugh, meanwhile, had lugged over his stones and laid them out.

"It makes a triangle. 1 plus 2 plus 3, is 6," he said, brushing the dirt off his hands.

Anne had brought a piece of honeycomb. She was passing out pieces to her friends when Sarah passed by on her way back to the castle. She saw all the flowers and smiled to think how well her friends had taken up her challenge.

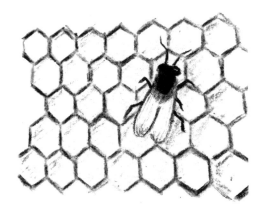

Sarah waved to her friends, calling out, "Be sure to ask Sir Hexagonal about the Crystal Cave."

One sunny day, while the children were doing the String Thing, a knight appeared.

"Dear children, Sarah was not exaggerating. You really are true students of mathematics."

"Ii's Sir Hexagonal," the children whispered to each other.

"Tell us about the Crystal Cave," Nick called out, jumping up and down.

"Ah, yes, the Crystal Cave", said Sir Hexagonal. "It was like this. As I was riding through the moonlit night, I caught a glimpse of purple light dancing in a cleft in the rock. I climbed upward until I came upon a cave heaped with purple crystals; amethysts they were. Looking carefully, I discovered that they were six-sided. Perhaps it was because of my devotion to the number six that I was granted entrance to that marvelous place. As I was leaving the cave, I saw snow beginning to fall across the moon, and across the purple light from the cave. The snow crystals as they fell, glowed with that same mysterious light."

Hearing the story, the children's faces seemed to share that glow.

The knight took a pouch from his belt, reached in, and gave one amethyst point to each child.

"These are for you," he said.

A diamond or a ruby wouldn't have been more precious to them.

SEVEN

"So, Sir Hexagonal did tell you about the crystal cave," Sarah said, when she next passed by the meadow.

"Well, Sir Septimo had quite an experience, himself, you know."

"What was that?" asked Rosemary, eagerly.

"He rode his horse right into a rainbow."

The children were puzzled.

"What do you mean, rode into a rainbow?" asked Lark.

"I know it sounds strange, but each color showered him in its light. Imagine yourself being completely surrounded by red or orange, or yellow, or green, or blue, or purple."

"I still don't understand," Lark said.

"Well, imagine yourself being surrounded by red. Everything is red, everything. Now close your eyes."

The children closed their eyes and really did imagine what that was like.

"Well, how was it?" asked Sarah.

"Red is very strong. It was almost scary," said Peter.

"It sure was," agreed Mary."

"It was interesting to see everything red, but I did long for the other colors, too," said Lark.

"How about blue?" asked Sarah.

"Well," answered Rosemary. "That's like swimming in the pond when the sky is very blue."

"But the trees, cows, birds, everything has to be blue, right, Sarah?" said Mary.

"That's right," said Sarah. "We can try this another time. I have to go soon."

"Could you just finish up the story of Sir Septimo before you go," asked Lark.

"Sure. It is important to know that when it was time for Sir Septimo to return for the feast, it was the Dipper, with its seven stars, that showed him the way back home. A special star in the Dipper pointed him to the North."

After Sarah had related the story of Sir Septimo, it became very quiet.

At last, Daniel spoke.

"Imagine that the Dipper, which we have seen so often above us, points us northward. It guided Sir Septimo back to King Maximo's court, and it can guide anyone who really looks for it. Maybe one day we'll go adventuring, too."

"Yes, and this knowledge is all of ours to use," replied Sarah, as she carefully placed six pennies around a seventh. "Look how perfectly they touch each other."

"And look at the pattern it makes between them," added Rosemary excitedly.

"That's interesting," said Nick. "What is it?"

"It's the way Sir Septimo arranged the buns on the table at the feast. Maybe it's six becoming seven," Sarah mused.

What was it Joccomo said about Sir Septimo?" asked Elizabeth.

"Well, Joccomo said:

Seven we know in the rainbow

The stars in the Dipper

The days of the week;

Seven is counted as

6 plus 1

5 plus 2

4 plus 3

"Hmmm," said Hugh, thoughtfully.

After Sarah had left to return to the castle, Hugh fetched his round stones and laid them out in a line. Pointing to each in turn, he called them *Monday, Tuesday, Wednesday, Thursday, Friday, Saturday, and Sunday.*

Robin stepped up with mischief on his mind, "*Sunday, Saturday, Friday, Thursday, Wednesday, Tuesday, Monday*," he recited, as he stepped from one to the other.

"That sounds backwards," said Hugh.

"Exactly backwards," replied Robin, skipping around the Great Circle.

"I want to try it that way too," Hugh said.

"Let's see, Sunday, Saturday, Friday, Thursday, Wednesday, Tuesday, Monday," he said slowly.

"I like that," said Nick, "it makes time go backwards for a change."

"These are seven fine stones," said Anne, admiring their roundness. She took one stone and moved it away from the line.

"There, that's 6 and 1. And, here's 5 and 2. And now, 4 and 3." She looked at the stones. "It's still seven, just a different arrangement.

"It looks like there's more to do too," said Mary. "Let me try."

"All right, here's 3 and 4, 2 and 5, and 1 and 6. Still it doesn't seem done."

Anne moved the last stone together with the others. "None and seven. How's that?" she said.

Later that day, Hugh was thinking about the buns he'd heard about from the feast. He was looking at the seven stones, when he started to arrange them with one in the middle surrounded by the other six.

The others looked on while he hefted the large stones, admiring how they fit together so well.

Next day, Daniel was playing in the squares and triangles when he shouted, "Look at this! The triangle set on the square looks like a house."

"Yes, it does," said Lark.

And so it went.

"What about Bring-a-Thing?" Elizabeth called out. Let's do it tomorrow. Don't forget."

"We won't," chorused several children.

When they arrived the next day, the children were treated to a wonderful sight. Right in the middle of the Great Circle, someone had laid out a rainbow arc made entirely of flower petals. Well, almost. Instead of green petals, there were leaves.

"Who brought these lovely petals?" asked Mary.

"I did," said Anne quietly. "I took it on as a beautiful challenge."

"It is curious, isn't it," said Daniel. "Leaves are green, but not flowers."

"They are when they're budding, but not when they've bloomed," said Lark.

"The String Thing?" called Elizabeth, but even as she spoke, she sounded a bit doubtful.

Try as they might, the children couldn't make it work.

"How would we make seven points on the circle?" Nick wondered.

"Well," said Mary, "we know how far apart the points were for all the other numbers so far. The spaces get closer and closer to each other. So with seven, they must be just a bit closer than with six. And of course, evenly spaced."

"That's it!" said Jessica. "Let's do it!"

It wasn't long before there were quite a few circles with seven evenly spaced points.

"It's easy to connect the points on the outside," said Lark, "but how are we ever going to get a star?"

"I've found it!" exclaimed Anne after a time, as excited as she ever got. "I just tried connecting every other point, and it worked. It couldn't have been simpler."

"Hooray for Anne!" the children cried.

Mary, who sang in the church choir, began singing notes that went up and down the scale. "Do, Re, Mi, Fa, So, La, Ti, Do. This is my Bring-a-Thing," she said.

"That's eight, not seven," said Robin. "I counted."

"Yes," replied Mary patiently, "only *Do* repeats itself at the top of the scale. Did you hear that?"

"I guess you're right," Robin had to admit, after he'd thought about it.

As they were following Mary's lead, singing the scales, a dark-haired knight rode up. They could all recognize the Great Dipper and the rainbow on his shield, and they nodded to each other.

"But what is this?" he gasped, noticing the rainbow of flowers. "Wonder of wonders, this reminds me of my great adventure!"

"Yes, we know. Sarah told us all about it," Elizabeth responded.

"It was as if you had ridden through a shower of all the colors of the rainbow, wasn't it."

The knight nodded, smiling. "Well, yes, it was."

Sir Septimo reached into a small pouch he was carrying and placed seven pieces of colored glass onto a white cloth in rainbow order.

"My friend who makes the stained glass windows for the cathedral gave these to me," Sir Septimo said. "I no longer have need of them, for I have only to shut my eyes and I can see the colors surrounding me. I want you to have them."

"Let's agree to keep them in our secret place, and never tell anyone else," said Peter, after Sir Septimo had left. They all agreed they would.

A few days later, Andrew was working with his barrel hoops. Nearly every day he made the circles taking a bite out of each other. This day, however, he had a hunch. He laid the hoop above the other two circles and made the third circle pass right through the middle.

The other children stood admiring it for a long while. "

Why it's seven little kingdoms!" shouted Rosemary. "What fun! I shall visit every one." And she proceeded to hop lightly through every space, without touching a single line.

Andrew found a bare patch near the Great Oak where he etched it again. This became a favorite game. It was considered lucky if you stepped into each kingdom without touching a line.

EIGHT

After Sarah had retold the story of Sir Otto, the children were quiet for a time, then Mary spoke.

"So, Sir Otto figured out that the whole castle was built according to an eight-sided figure?"

"You really mean that even the towers were eight-sided?" asked Nick.

"Yes," replied Sarah, "Sir Otto called them octagons. There was an octagonal tower at each of the corners of the octagonal castle."

"How did Sir Otto guess this?" asked Nick.

"Well, it started with the stick. Remember how he picked up a stick and snapped it in half; then snapped the halves in half; and then the quarters in half?"

"You mean like this," said Robin, picking up a hazel twig. Everyone was a bit surprised at how expertly Robin snapped the twig, ending up with eight equal pieces.

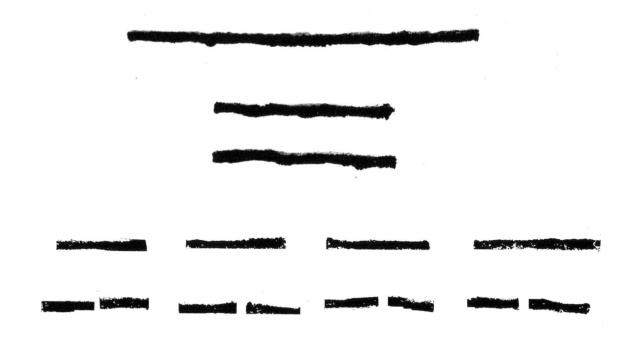

Robin, quickly laid four of the pieces in a square. It was not quite so easy to lay the second square atop the first, however.

Straightaway, Robin's friends started selecting the straightest twigs in order to try themselves.

"There's nothing better than snapping a good twig," said Nick.

"Agreed," said Lark.

It wasn't as easy as it looked, however, and the children had to pay attention to what they were doing.

Hugh, meanwhile, had gone off to the side, playing with the stick squares.

"Is this what Sir Otto made?" he asked shyly, showing two squares, one atop the other, the top one partly turned.

"Why, yes it was," replied Sarah.

"Look how carefully you've made that," said Anne, admiringly, "you have eight triangles sticking out, all exactly the same size. It's beautiful!"

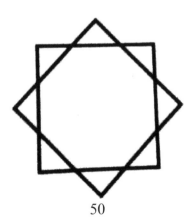

Others, who were having trouble breaking the sticks evenly, went over to the pile of squares and began making the shape for themselves.

Then, one by one, they set about drawing the figure in the dirt within the Great Circle. Most of them couldn't quite get it to work. They'd gotten good at making the first square, but the turned one was hard. They'd learned by now, though, to give their best effort, and then to leave off and try again later.

Jessica, of course, was one of those who could draw it.

"Well done, Jessica," complimented Daniel, looking thoughtfully at her figure.

"Wait a second, I think I see something. The angles of the second square lie right over the middle of the sides of the first square. And, I also can picture how big each triangle should be."

Carefully, Daniel drew his best square, and then he made a dot over the middle of each side.

"Now I only need to connect the dots."

When he'd finished the second square, he stood up and looked at it with satisfaction.

"Nice going," said Jessica enthusiastically. "It's great, the way you figured it out!"

"I just opened my eyes," replied Daniel.

Daniel's explanation encouraged the others. They went at it with renewed enthusiasm until most had done it. Then Andrew took a stick and inscribed it in the Great Circle.

"And I'll bet there was a wall around the castle," said Anne, remembering the hexagon. She took the stick and connected the eight points.

"There," she said, standing with hands on hips.

No one had noticed Sir Otto walking up.

"For some reason this looks quite familiar to me," he said laughing.

"Then you must be Sir Otto," said Rosemary confidently.

"Sir Otto, is this what the castle looked like?" asked Andrew.

"Why, yes, basically."

"I know what your third challenge was," said Nick. "You had to win a game of chess."

"That's right," said Sir Otto, nodding his head.

"Can you show us how to play?" asked Jessica.

"I can make a start. Of course, we need the chess board," said Sir Otto.

First he drew a square in the dirt. Then he divided it in half, with a line running from top to bottom. Next, he drew a line across the middle, from left to right.

"Now, a top to bottom line on either side of the middle line. And the same going crossways," said Sir Otto.

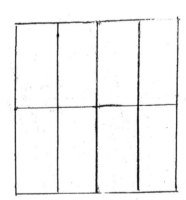 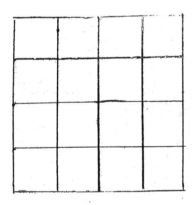

"That's sixteen," called Robin.

"Right you are," said Sir Otto.

"Now, here's the hardest part, you have to concentrate. We need each square to be divided into four squares. There are several ways, but the easiest way is this. Four more lines top to bottom, evenly spaced. The same going across. There. Takes practice."

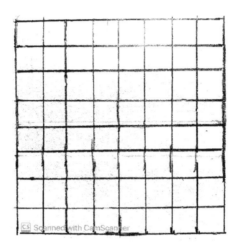

"Let's see," observed Nick, "that's eight each direction... Hmmm. I'm guessing, but I think that's sixty-four spaces."

Hugh looked up. He'd only gotten to eight.

"You were right, Nick," Hugh said after a time.

Sir Otto opened his pouch and poured chess pieces onto the ground. "I carved them myself from soapstone," he said.

The children were fascinated by the beautifully carved chess pieces.

"Can you teach us how to play?" asked Nick?

"Tell you what, I will come back another time. In the meanwhile, practice making those chessboards."

"Oh, and here," said the knight, handing a strip of metal down from his horse.

"Something to remember me by. Just bend it into a bracelet."

The children waved happily as Sir Otto rode off.

NINE

Sarah had just finished telling the story of Sir Thrice-Thrice.

"Sarah, did you say that Sir Thrice-Thrice was the younger brother of Sir Thrice?" asked Mary.

"Yes," Sarah replied. "He was so good-natured, barely more than a lad. He was fun, as much fun as, well, Tic-Tac-Toe!

When he laid out nine hazelnuts, I was surprised at what I saw. After all, three is an odd number, and three threes also make an odd number, right, nine. Yet, what it made was a perfect square, and squares are even, the same on all four sides, right!" Sarah said, as she laid out the three rows of three.

"Acorns work as well as hazelnuts," said Lark, laying nine of them out in a square.

"The chessboard is also a perfect square, isn't it?" Daniel said. "Only there are eight to a side."

"That's right!" Nick agreed.

"Did Sir Thrice-Thrice ever show the other knights what was written on his magic square?" asked Mary.

"Of course he did," replied Sarah. "They wouldn't stop pestering him until he did."

"How was it, anyway?" asked Anna.

"Well, you remember the Tic-Tac -Toe form," said Sarah. "What you have to do is fill it in using the numbers 1 to 9, but only one time each, no repeats. Down, across, and on a slant, the three numbers must add up to the same thing."

"Which number?" asked Lark, full of anticipation.

"Oh," said Sarah. "Sir Thrice-Thrice wouldn't tell, not at first, anyway."

"Just tell us," said Jessica. "I can't wait to get started."

"All right," said Sarah reluctantly, "it was fifteen."

"Fifteen, good," said Andrew. "Let's get to work."

Before you knew it, there was a Tic -Tac-Toe figure in front of each of the children, and all were busy filling in numbers.

"I've got it!" called Daniel, grinning proudly.

"Let's see," said Elizabeth.

"Not on your life," Daniel objected, covering up his work. "That would take all the fun out of it. Let's agree to work it out for ourselves, otherwise we'll lose a great chance to learn. If you don't get it after you've tried, I'll give you a hint, okay?"

A few had found the solution, but most were still struggling, when Nick asked for a clue.

"All right," said Daniel, "try putting a five in the middle."

Back to work they went. Some got it, and others didn't. By the next day, everyone had found the answer.

2	7	6
9	5	1
4	3	8

One day the children arrived to find Andrew putting the finishing touches on a magic square he had carved into a block of wood. As they were admiring it, a young knight leapt down from his horse, landing lightly.

"Well, well, the magic square. It seems that you've been very busy."

Rosemary started to say something, but all the others looked at her, and then they all laughed.

"Now, what's that you're doing, my good fellow?" the young knight called to Nick. Nick was unusually quiet. He'd had a hunch, and now he was playing with the stick triangles.

Nick laid three triangles, one atop the other and adjusted them a bit.

 "You've done it," said Sir Thrice-Thrice.

And sure enough, Nick had made a star with nine evenly spaced points.

Many of the children were attempting to draw this in the Great Circle.

In the mean time, Hugh was carrying over his stones. One by one he laid them out in a square.

"Very nicely done," said Sir Thrice-Thrice.

Now, watch this," said the young knight. Taking his sword, he drew a line separating three stones off from one corner.

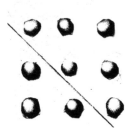

The children watched intently, then, suddenly, Anne called out, "A triangle of three and a triangle of six. Isn't it lovely!"

"Yes, isn't it," replied the knight.

Sir Thrice-Thrice looked over at the stacks of triangles. He walked over and picked some up. Working quickly he arranged them in a pattern.

"It's the Four-In-One Triangle," several children called out, a bit disappointed, somehow.

"I'm not done," said the young knight, as he went on, laying down yet another row.

"Now look at this, my friends. What do you see?"

"It's a Nine-In-One Triangle," they shouted.

"Hooray for Sir Thrice-Thrice!" they cheered.

"There's one last thing I wanted to show you," said Sir Thrice-Thrice. "Do you see the stones our friend has arranged in such a nice square? Well, I'm going to move a few.

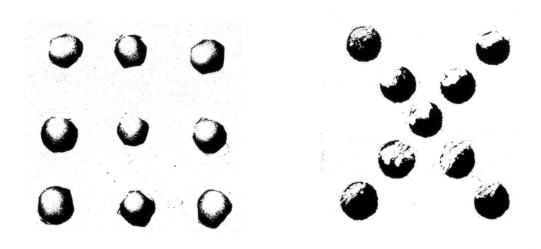

"Voila!" said the young knight with a wave.

"I'm certain that Sir Ten will like what I've just done."

"You changed it completely by moving just four stones," said Daniel, quite impressed.

"Yes, but which four?" asked Robin, who wasn't watching carefully.

"Don't worry, you'll get it, sooner or later, Robin," said Mary.

The knight was already walking toward his horse. He looked back over his shoulder.

"Imagine," he called out. "Just imagine."

TEN

Sarah found herself, more and more, enjoying her time visiting with her old friends. She was learning as much from them as they were from her.

Sarah began:

"Sir Ten was the oldest of the knights. The younger knights liked to tease him, good naturedly, of course. Sir Ten had made it clear that ten was a very useful number for counting. Everyone knew he was right. 'That's for sir-ten,' they would say."

Sir Ten told how one day he rode down into a fog-shrouded valley. As the fog lifted, he began to make out lines of men, arranged in such an orderly manner that he had to marvel. So he asked the officer in charge how he got them to be so orderly.

The officer, who was near-sighted had decided that ten was a good number of men for each line. When they stood in a row he had the first hold up his arm, then the second and the, third. As he didn't see so well, he made sure the fifth held up his hand like this. The V-shape became five, and then he knew the one in front of him was four. Likewise, the one after was six, the next was seven, and the next was eight. Now it became really hard for him to see, so he had the tenth man raise both his arms and make an X with them. Then he knew that the one before him was nine.

The numbers went like this," said Sarah, writing them in the dirt:

$$\text{I} \quad \text{II} \quad \text{III} \quad \text{IV} \quad \text{V} \quad \text{VI} \quad \text{VII} \quad \text{VIII} \quad \text{IX} \quad \text{X}$$

After Sarah had told the story of Sir Ten, the children set to work writing the unusual numbers in the dirt of the Great Circle.

Next day Hugh brought out a soldier he'd made of clay from the creek. It was a simple shape, little more than a lump. What was special was the piece of bark pressed into the front for a shield, and, on the right side, a twig serving as a spear. Soon all the children had fetched clay and were busy following Hugh's example.

With so many hands at work, it wasn't long before they had five lines of soldiers. They were working so intently on their figures that they hardly noticed the gray-haired knight with side-whiskers slowly climbing down from his horse.

"Spent a lot of time in the saddle and sleeping on the ground. The bones are a bit stiff," said the knight in a hoarse voice.

"That's for Sir Ten," laughed Robin as he ran and skipped around the Great Circle.

Sir Ten noticed the clay soldiers right away.

"Fine work!" he said. "Let's see how many lines you have. One, two, three, four, five lines. Well, that makes fifty, and fifty in Roman numerals is written as the capital letter D."

"Yes, and we hope to have a hundred by tomorrow," said Andrew proudly.

"Marvelous! Now remember, when you reach a hundred you will write that with a C. That stands for 'century'. That's what they called a group of a hundred soldiers. It can also mean a hundred years."

"Now, boys and girls, I'm going to test you. I will say a number, and you will write the Roman numeral for it. Ready?"

Sir Ten said a number, and the children wrote it in the dirt using the Roman numerals. They were all very excited to show what they'd learned.

Sir Ten gave them problem after problem. They quickly saw that it was not so easy to add the Roman numerals, not to mention take away. It seemed Sir Ten had grown tired.

"Dear boys and girls, I think Sir Double Digit was right when he said that this way of counting no longer serves us so well. It's time for me to move on.

Hugh, meanwhile, had taken his stones and made a triangle with ten stones- four, then three, then two, then one. Sir Ten noticed the beautiful triangle and smiled.

Then Sir Ten slowly mounted his horse, waved to the children, and rode off.

ELEVEN

"Was Sir Doubledigit impressed by all the gold the king had?" asked Mary.

"Not really," replied Sarah. "In fact, he found it quite silly that the king had made his gold into heavy bars. What was he going to do with it, after all? What really impressed Sir Doubledigit was the way two could be worth more than seven."

"You mean, if the two is in the tens place and the seven is in the ones place," said Nick, recalling what Sarah had explained to them. "The two stands for two tens, and the seven stands for seven ones, doesn't it."

"Exactly," replied Sarah, happy that her friends could share so nicely in her learning. "That's called place value. The king's clerks were very careful to line the numerals up, and then it was very easy to add and to subtract."

The children understood place value.

"It just makes sense," said Mary.

The others agreed.

"But what is a numeral, asked Rosemary.

"A numeral," answered Sarah, "is what we use to write numbers. Some people just call them numbers, but that's not quite right. The first three are 1, 2, and 3. Can you guess what the other ones are?"

"I know," said Elizabeth, "4,5,6,7,8, 9 and 10."

"Well, that's quite good, said Sarah, "but we already have the one that you see in ten."

"Oh," said Elizabeth, "it really is quite simple."

"I wish I didn't, but I have to go now," said Sarah. "Till next time."

"Good-bye, Sarah," the children chorused cheerfully as she walked off down the road to the castle.

The children set about copying what Sarah had drawn of Sir Double Digit's shield.

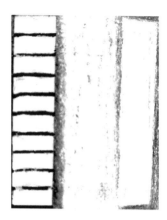

"Sir Double Digit's shield really shows that the place you put a numeral tells how much it is worth," said Mary.

"Yes," agreed Elizabeth, "the one on the right is one single bar, while the one on the left stands for one stack of ten bars."

The children didn't notice the knight who had walked up quietly behind them.

"What's five 10s and three 1s?" he asked.

The children were startled, but they chorused, "Fifty three."

By now, it didn't seem out of the ordinary for a knight to appear.

"Nine tens and five ones?" he continued.

"Ninety-five," they again chorused.

"Well, then, if you have 32 and you add 22, how much is that?" asked the knight.

About half the children answered without flinching, "54."

"I still don't quite know how to do this," said Anne. "I'm still a bit confused."

"Well," said Mary, "2 ones and 2 ones are 4 ones, while 2 tens and 3 tens are 50. Fifty and four is fifty-four."

"Now I see," said Anne, happily.

"If you keep the numbers in their proper columns, you'll have no problems, said Sir Double Digit. "I'm sure Sarah will soon show you about 'carrying'."

Sir Doubledigit took some pieces of wood out of his pouch. They were carved to look just like bars of gold.

"I want you to have these," he said, "to remember that where a numeral is placed tells how much it is worth."

TWELVE

The next time the children encountered Sarah, she had just witnessed the most amazing thing. Sir Duzen had presented his gift, twelve balls, clustered perfectly around a central ball. "You are the one in the middle, dear King Maximo," he had said.

"Without your question, we would not have made our marvelous discoveries."

No one, it seemed, could figure out how it was that the balls had clung together as they did, and Sir Duzen was not telling. He simply said that it was something that had always been. The children tried to imagine this, but they couldn't. Of course, they could picture a ball in the center with a lot of other balls clustered around it, but that was all.

One day, Hugh had an idea. He was just going to start in making balls out of clay. The problem was that they were all slightly different sizes. Then he had another idea, to make a clay bar and to cut it up into 13 equal pieces, like a loaf of bread. This way, when he rolled them into balls, they would all turn out to be the same size. It worked! Then Hugh laid six into place around the one in the middle. "Like the buns," he said. "That is seven, and now I need six more. Hmmm, that's two triangles."

He tried it, and it worked. And, they stuck together!

The children were so proud of Hugh.

"Hugh," said Elizabeth, "you just set about working, and the solution found you."

Meanwhile, Hugh had set the figure atop a stump. From time to time, the children found themselves gazing at it in wonderment. The more they looked, the more they saw in it.

The next time Sarah visited, Elizabeth said, "Sir Duzen's gift to King Maximo certainly was exciting, but wasn't there more that Sir Duzen said at the feast?"

"The most exciting thing about Sir Duzen was that he didn't leave his room when he went on his quest," said Sarah, much to the amazement of her friends.

"What do you mean, Sarah?" asked Mary. "How can that be?"

"Well, Sir Duzen had decided to pass his year in study and contemplation. He had his food brought to him secretly. One night, there appeared to him a woman, beautiful beyond compare. She tossed him a glowing ball that just hung in the air. The ball had twelve sides, and each side was a pentagon. She never returned, but the ball did, every night. The amazing thing was that he could look through the sides of the ball as if they were windows. He called them 'wonder windows', and through them he could look on the same thing in twelve different ways.

The children were silent, as Sarah went on.

"Oh yes, Sir Duzen was grand. Sir Duzen said that what he was he owed to the other Number Knights."

"For one thing, five has a special connection with twelve," said Sarah. "Sir Duzen realized that the ball which the lady had tossed him had 12 sides, and that each side was a pentagon."

"In his own way, Sir Duzen was like a king," said Sarah. "Somehow he was connected to all of the numbers."

"We have seen it on the Great Circle!" shouted Robin, jumping up and down. "Do you remember the String Thing from long ago?

"Oh, yeah," voiced Nick. Let's do it."

Out came the string, and around the circle it flew. By now skipping fives was easy for them.

"Is it a star, or is it a sun?" Rosemary asked finally. They all laughed.

"What's the difference?" called Nick.

As they were finishing up, a stately knight in a purple cape rode up.

"Sir Duzen," the children gasped in chorus.

"Yes, I am Sir Duzen," the knight said softly.

"Who was the lady," Nick asked urgently, "won't you please tell us?"

"The lady, I believe, was Sophia, or Wisdom. You may not see her, but you know she is there, whenever you sincerely seek to learn."

"Sir Duzen,"asked Nick, "What can we do to be better?"

Sir Duzen listened, then answered thoughtfully, "Whenever you really listen to what someone else is saying, or try to understand them, you are becoming wiser. Each time you view the world with new eyes, you are growing taller. I was fortunate to be granted the gift of looking through the twelve wonder windows."

The knight had gazed into the distance for a moment, when suddenly he noticed Hugh's figure on the stump.

"Why, it's remarkable, you've solved my problem!" the knight said, his eyes lighting up. "I haven't got any more magnetic iron balls, but I wanted to make a special gift to the other knights. Now you've shown me that I can make them in clay. How can I thank you?"

"You already have," cried Sarah, "you, and all of the Number Knights. You have given us far more than we will ever, ever know."

Sarah looked at her friends, and they looked back at her. Then they looked at one another, and smiled.

THE END

Postscript

The children, oh the children. Well, they all went on to do different things in their lives, but they did not forgot Sarah, or the Number Knights.

The Unmanual

Sarah and the Number Knights is a manual in story form. Although I am committed to having any instructions come from the mouths of the characters in the story, I do recognize that teachers and parents have much on their plates, so I have also included more explicit indications.

The suggested activities follow the course of the story. The best use of this work in my view would be to treat it as a teaching play in which children can live into the imaginations provided by the story and to make their own discoveries. Review and repetition are keys to this form of learning. An area, designated by a round rug, could serve as a focal point the way the Great Circle in the story does. Materials such as sticks, hoops, balls, clay, etc. can be left out for the children's use. Slates or paper may be used for doodling. Bringing in materials and activities from previous chapters is very strengthening. This story involves "slow learning", which results in deep learning.

Please omit any of the activities that don't fit into your teaching plan. And, add any activities you might develop based on your own interactions with the numbers, and with the children. The age of the children will help determine the way in which you present the story and the activities. The story works well with children of varying ages in the same group as well.

TWELVE, naturally, is the perfect number of children to work with in bringing this story to life. In treating the material as if it were a play, you would have Sarah plus the eleven knights (Sir Pentagonal is away, remember). With a full class of 24 or more there could be two casts, with the child roles alternating with Sarah's and the Number Knights' roles.

NOTE: If you lack the requisite number of children to replicate the circle of twelve, consider drawing a circle on a 1"X12" pine board. Mark 12 equidistant points like on a clock face. (See 12-Division of a Circle below.) Then drive small nails into each point. This works especially well for re-enacting the String Thing. Do this by wrapping the string around the nails to create the various geometric forms. Taking it one step further, one can drill 12 holes part way through the board using a spade bit the same diameter as the base of wooden peg dolls. The dolls may then be inserted into the holes to represent the children in the story. 7/8" diameter works well.

Faces, hair, clothes, etc. can be applied to make the dolls more life-like, and to further engage the imagination. Finally, features of the meadow landscape can be painted on the board to create a setting for the story to unfold in. Even in a full class of children, individuals and small groups with gather around "the meadow" at various times, and re-enact parts of the story.

Note: It may be helpful to assign places on the Great Circle for specific characters. . While this ordering is somewhat arbitrary and not absolutely necessary, it could make the proceedings more orderly. A possible order would be: 0)Elizabeth (at top); 1)Mary; 2)Daniel; 3)Andrew; 4)Jessica; 5)Anne; 6)Hugh; 7)Rosemary; 8)Nick; 9)Peter; 10)Lark; 11)Robin; 12)Elizabeth again.

Robin is a rascal; Jessica and Andrew are take charge types; Rosemary is the youngest and quite lively; Hugh is methodical and slow-moving; Mary is strong and steady, and also musical; Anne is gentle and aesthetic; Nick is quick-thinking and observant; Daniel is steady; Peter is playful; Elizabeth is serious; Lark is light-hearted. These are just quick characterizations. For those working with temperaments, again roughly speaking: Choleric-Andrew and Jessica; Phlegmatic-Hugh and Anne; Melancholic- Mary, Nick, Daniel, Elizabeth; Sanguine-Lark, Robin, Rosemary, Peter.

It simplifies things if the children go to the same place on the Great Circle each time.

12-Division of a Circle (for the above project)

Use a compass to draw a circle. Keeping the same radius, place the point of the compass on the top of the circle. Then draw a small arc that intersects the circumference. Put the point of the compass on this intersection, and repeat until you have 6 equally spaced "intersections." Select 2 adjacent intersections and, from each of them, draw an arc outside the circumference so that the 2 arcs intersect, making a small X. Draw a very light line from the X to the center of the circle. This line will bisect one of the 6 arcs of

the circle. Repeat the initial process until you have 12 points on the circle.

Basic Materials:

TOOL KIT
A tool kit is available containing most of the materials needed to carry out the activities in this book.
For more information please go to http://www.lmntreepress and look beside
Sarah and the Number Knights under Math Stories.

Playground ball

Sketch pads or main lesson books to record activities and draw illustrations

Crayons and pencils

2 balls of thick yarn or cord about 3" in diameter

Straight twigs of similar dimensions (4)

Thin doweling 20", 24", 36", 48"long, 3/16 in. diameter; from hardware store or lumber yard

Craft or popsicle sticks (50-100)

Low heat glue gun

Small slate or chalkboard (optional) ; chalk

Clay- (recommended Sargent art non-hardening modeling clay)

Paper and scissors

*More specific materials are listed chapter by chapter in the Unmanual.

Drawing the Shields (Coats of Arms)

Children derive great pleasure from drawing the shields (coats of arms) accompanying the story of *King Maximo and the Number Knights.* Perhaps they have alreadydrawn them in conjunction with the story. If not, they may draw them while they are participating in the story of *Sarah and the Number Knights.*

The children want them to look good, so:

Use good quality paper. An 11"X14" sketch pad works well. Before drawing the shield, plan and practice it. It is best if the shield covers most of the paper and is nicely centered. Draw it first using "the phantom," the term I use for drawing without making contact, hovering just above the paper. Use crayons that have a little drag so the children can work slowly and carefully.

While the appearance of the shields in King Maximo may benefit aesthetically from the flourish of the curve on the top, drawing this way may present too great a challenge for some children. Therefore, I suggest a modification, a straight line at the top, at least at first.

Start about 2" from the top of the paper, and about 1" from the left edge. Demonstrate where it will stop, about 1" from the right edge. First use the phantom and then draw slowly and carefully. Make sure the line runs parallel to the top of the paper. 'Railroad tracks' is a good term for parallel.

Ask the children to find the mid-point of the top line and then drop down, using the phantom, to a point about 2" from the bottom of the paper. Make a light mark.

Draw a line straight down from the end of the top line, parallel to side of the paper, until you are about half way to the bottom. Then, aiming for the point, gradually curve the line until it meets the point. Repeat on the other side. Again, use the phantom first.

This is the basic shield form. It can be modified, but it should be mastered before variations are attempted.

Centering also makes a difference in drawing the symbols on the shields. It is strengthening for the children to develop a sense for this, an aesthetic sense. In the case of the shields for 1 & 12, for eg., it makes a difference if the 12 rays are not drawn randomly, but rather, first drawn in the four compass directions. Each quadrant may then be divided into 3 parts. It is also more artistic to draw the rays with space left between them and the central disc.

Each shield, when observed carefully, has some characteristics for the teacher or parent to point out, which will help the children to draw them successfully. It is important to draw them yourself first so that you can share your experience.

As suggested in the story, the shields may sometimes be made with flower petals, leaves, bits of colored paper, beads, etc.

The main thing is to enjoy this experience. Perhaps the shields will line the wall of a classroom or a bedroom, as they did the wall of the Great Hall at King Maximo's castle.

ONE

Materials:

Hula hoops; barrel hoops from wineries or landscape supply are even better

Staff-like stick (mop or broom handle handle will do)

2 metal rings about 1" diameter (large enough for staff to fit through); from hardware store

String (as long as the radius of the circle you want to make); 6 ft. works well

Thin branch or twig about 2 ft. long

Playground ball

Activities:

One is about unity.

Sun- in-the-Middle- If the description in the story doesn't suffice, look up the game of *Spud*. The former is based on the latter, just with a more evocative name.

Have children run off, and then come back and reform the circle. Expand the circle. Contract the circle. Rotate the circle. Pass the ball around the circle (while counting or saying a verse). Move the circle to different places. Holding hands may help initially. The ultimate might be to move the circle while rotating it and passing a ball. Practice is key. That, and visualizing the round disc in the center.

Bring-a-Thing- Have children bring circular and spherical objects as suggested in the story.

Free-hand drawing-Practice drawing free hand circles. Begin by doing the 'phantom', drawing it just over the paper, without applying the crayon or pencil. In drawing circles it is helpful to be mindful of where the center lies. The circle cuts out a disc.

The Bird's Nest In the Bramble Bush- To prepare for drawing the circle, you might begin by scribbling in a loop-de-loop fashion. Use the image of a bramble bush, randomly scribbling, but always with a clockwise hand movement. Gradually arrive at the circle, the nest, from out of this movement.

Hoops provide a good springboard into hula-hoop activities, hoop rolling, and even free gymnastics.

Playground chalk may substitute for a stick when constructing the Great Circle with the string compass, especially if doing it on asphalt or concrete. Make smaller circles using shorter lengths of string.

NOTE: Reciting the poem while passing the ball may be carried over to any or all of the poems. Repetition over a number of days is essential. Try emphasizing different words, phrasing, and tempos as the character of Joccomo might do.

Bring-a-Thing may also be done in relation to all of the numbers. Mary introduces the notion of singing the poems, which were composed using a pentatonic flute. Any or all of the other poems can be learned in a similar way through simple repetition. Songs are to be found at the back of this book. Learning even a few of the songs introduces the musical element into the work.

TWO

Materials:

Small rubber balls, juggling balls, bean bags, or even apples

Paper circles, ready-made or cut out

Bits of paper, leaves, beans, flower petals, etc. (to fill in the portions of the shield)

Hula hoops or barrel hoops; Sir Owen's larger than life "compass" may also be used to construct other circles.

Activities:

Two is about duality, polarity.

Children pair up and recite, passing objects in a rhythmical way. A playground ball may be bounced back and forth, as well. Two familiar verses are: One, two, Buckle my shoe/Three, four, Shut the door/Five, six, Pick up sticks/Seven, eight, Lay them straight/ Nine, ten, A good fat hen... or

1 and 1 are 2, that's for me and you/ 2 and 2 are 4, that's a couple more/ 3 and 3 are 6, barley sugar sticks/ 4 and 4 are 8, tumblers at the gate/ 5 and 5 are 10, bold sea-faring men... (toss on underlines)

Hugh's Two-person Saw Activity-*Standing opposite each other toe-to-toe, #1 holds LEFT THUMB straight up; #2 wraps 4 fingers of RT HAND around the thumb, sticking own thumb straight up; now #1 wraps 4 fingers of own RT HAND around #2's thumb, and finally #2 wraps 4 fingers of LEFT HAND around #1's thumb. Having done this they proceed to push and pull alternately, reciprocally, in the gesture of the two-person saw.*

Bring language arts into math study-This is an opportunity to connect math with language arts, calling attention to opposites (antonyms) in particular,. Try omitting some of the verses from the story and have students come up with their own. This is a casual way of creating simple poems, too.

Bring-a-Thing- Anything that comes in pairs; bicycles, glasses, binoculars, gloves, shoes, socks, etc. Poems having to do with contrasts may also be studied.

Highlight the bilateral symmetry of the body.

Recreating Sir Twain's shield provides an opportunity to show how different pairings contrast with each other, complement each other, or even create something new together. Some combinations are "more beautiful" than others.

The original version of the shield contained the Yin-Yang symbol. I changed it because it proved a bit too hard for many of the younger children to draw. Older children working with this material might attempt it.

Make a circle using Sir Owen's larger than life "compass". Find any point on the circumference and place the staff's point there to create a second circle. When making the first circle, demonstrate that the circle is twice as wide as the string is long, in other words, that the diameter is twice the radius. These terms are best held back with younger children, though.

It is quite difficult for the younger child to draw two intersecting circles free hand. Some can do it, but that is the exception. The arc of one circle passes through the center of the other. Place the point staff on the circumference of the first circle at any place and draw the second circle. Resist the temptation to use a hand-held compass with younger children.

Find the "Almond" Sir Twain refers to, made from intersecting circle. Tracing them with a yoghurt lid, for example, or find circles ready-made. Notice that the *intersection* of the two circles recalls the Venn Diagram. Glass beads, pebbles, sand, or bits of paper can highlight this overlap. In autumn, leaves of different colors work well.

Coloring or painting a blue circle and a red circle results in a purple intersection.

Discover the line that runs between the centers of the two circles. Without referring to it as the radius, notice how the line running between the two centers does in fact serve as the radius for both circles at once. This has been referred to as "the birth of the line". We could simply say that "they share it".

A Story of Discovery

Years ago, while preparing to teach the bisection of a line segment to 7th graders, the heavy wooden board compass I was using to make small Xs above and below the line slipped, clearly leaving the trace of a large arc. I completed the arc, making a circle. I repeated this going the other direction, making another circle. The form created fascinated me. I felt I had discovered a secret garden hidden behind the wall of my traditional schooling. This may have been the decisive moment when this work woke up in me.

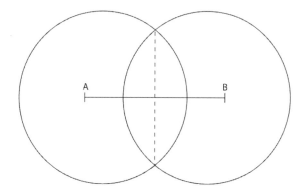

THREE

Materials:

3 straight twigs, or thin dowels of about the same length

Popsicle or craft sticks

Low heat glue gun

Ball of thick yarn or twine

Three-petaled flowers- trillium, iris and snowdrop are three of them

Three leaf clover or drawing of one

Activities:

The initial demonstration of forming a triangle may be done with sticks of roughly the same size. It's nice if children gather them themselves. Disposable chopsticks or thin dowels may be used as substitutes. The actual triangle may be the sticks themselves, or the area created in the center.

It's fun to act out the dialog about corners and angles.

The String Thing- Elizabeth and Mary act this out. If possible choose someone with mischievous tendencies to play Robin. Each child chooses a spot on the Great Circle as their go-to spot. Elizabeth gets to be at the top (0/12) because she has brought the string. Even though isosceles and scalene triangles are observed, it is refreshing to characterize them, but to leave the naming for a later grade.

As for "The Beautiful Triangle", there will be many opportunities later on for them to learn the term, 'equilateral triangle'. Resisting the temptation will ensure that they will learn it in a deeper way later on.

"Walking the triangle" gets the learning into the limbs. Any of the triangles can be "walked", as if sawing out a piece from the floor. There is an opportunity here to weave in skip-counting-2,4,6,8...3,6,9,12..., etc. as they walk the form, a lead-in to multiplication, or a review.

Bring-a-Thing is an opportunity to work with braiding, aspects of architecture, and so on. Three-ness can be seen in a 3-leaf clover, a footstool, and in all the various aspects listed in the story. Go over a section of the outline of a picture of a 3-leaf clover to find the shape of the numeral '3'.

Hugh makes a 'triangular number' with the stones. This theme will be carried on throughout the story.

To add a bit more magic (after all 1+2=3), take the interpenetrating circles (almond in the center) and do the following: starting at the top, at the point where the circles intersect, draw lines through the center of both circles, stopping when they touch the circumference at the bottom. Then connect these two points. Voila, two, the line, has become three, the triangle.

The Four-In-One Triangle- In the dirt, on the chalkboard or on the black top draw the Four-In-One Triangle. Have someone representing Sir Thrice hold a "sword" over each side in turn, asking to be told when the sword is right in the middle of the line. This develops powers of observation in the children. Connect the three points, thus creating the Four-In-One Triangle.

The Four-In-One Triangle may be further subdivided to get to a Sixteen-In-One triangle. Try different approaches to drawing this. Use as many lines as possible, or as few.

Lashing- By all means, try lashing sticks together. It is quite a challenging thing to do. Glueing craft sticks together provides a simple, doable way to represent the triangle archetype. Make sure the ends of the sticks line up together just right.

Tetrahedron- Sir Thrice goes to Thomas the Tinker to have tetrahedrons made, a solid composed of four equilateral triangles. Make the Four-In-One Triangle on stiff card. Score the edges of the center triangle, and then fold up the sides. Tape.

FOUR

Materials:

Four sticks of approximately the same length

Popsicle sticks or craft sticks

Low heat glue gun

String, or twist ties

Broomstick or long dowel

Activities:

Discuss various aspects of four-ness as it relates to construction, directions, seasons, baking, elements, etc.

Get down on all fours. Imagine the cow. Feel the solidity and stability of the position.

Lay out sticks to make squares and rectangles.

String Thing- Toss the ball of string to four random points around circle. The form will have four sides, but is not a square. By skipping every 3 spaces you get a square. Deduce this by the process of elimination. For eg. two cannot be used because four 2s are 8. Jumping three spaces gives a square. From the cardinal directions it will look like a diamond, but a shift in viewpoint reveals it is also a square. If you start at a point halfway between 1 and 2 (1 ½) and then skip three spaces it will look more like a square.

Using a glue gun, make squares with popsicle sticks. Line up the ends of the sticks so they join perfectly.

Practice drawing freehand squares. Show children how to sketch, drawing lightly at first, suggesting the square until you can get it right. Probably, even practicing drawing lightly will need to be practiced. Many children press down too hard and make mistakes they regret. Remember the Right Angles of Sir Foursquare.

Doodling- Ask the students to divide a square. At first, it appears that there are only a few ways to do so- 1) Horizontal line; 2) vertical line; 3) diagonal line. After a time someone will use two lines.

1. Divide the square with a vertical line and a horizontal line, a cross.

2. Divide the square with two diagonal lines.

3. Make both crosses within the square.

Find triangles within the squares, strengthening the sense that the numbers are interrelated.

The Four-in-One Square- A vertical and a horizontal line create four squares in one.

Making the numeral 4 - On the upper left hand quadrant of the Four-In-One Square, trace over the upper left vertical line, then the middle horizontal line three-quarters of the way, and finally the line that cuts the large square in half vertically. You have the numeral four.

The Staff-of-Uprightness- Hold a broomstick perpendicular to the ground. Ask a student to move the stick. Sufficient pressure must be applied in order to keep the stick from slipping out, and to make the point about the strength right angles provide.

Recall the various ways four makes things strong.

Hugh and Elizabeth count the triangles- Elizabeth has a sense of the virtue of multiplication; Hugh is still adding.

Fashion a ball of clay as large as is practicable. Using thumb and forefinger, press top and bottom and opposite sides. Then do the other two sides, and then the other. Keep at it until you have a cube.

Nick's Cube- Take six of the popsicle stick squares. Arrange 4 squares around a central square. Stand them upright and then fasten them with string, twisty ties, or drops of glue. Add a sixth square on top to complete the cube.

Bring-a-Thing may be continued. A tremendous variety of square objects may be brought in.

Sir Foursquare's Shield- Divide the shield into four quadrants representing the four elements. Lower right stands for earth. A mixture of dark colors can fill it in, or one could draw a crystal. Lower left is water, which may be represented by a series of wavy lines. Upper left represents air. A cloud shape hollowed out of surrounding blue suffices. Finally fire. Lay down a yellow background and bring in red flame forms on top of this. Simple symbols could also be used to illustrate the 4 elements, especially if drawing in the dirt.

SIR THRICE AND SIR FOURSQUARE GO RIDING

This chapter provides a wonderful opportunity to reinforce the idea that there are many ways to look at a given situation.

It is especially fun to act out this scene. Many children will want to be Sir Foursquare.

Mold a cube of clay, either individually or in a group. Or, imagine it. The pieces of clay used may vary widely in size. Start by rolling a ball and then press in from all sides alternately to shape the cube. This is an interesting exercise. The six sides are the result of pressure from six directions, left, right, top, bottom, front and back. They may also be viewed as three pairs of opposites. Thus an interconnection is made involving 2,3, and 6.

FIVE

Materials:

5-petaled flowers- (Rose family): columbine, buttercups, pansies, borage, periwinkle, geranium, primroses, etc., and, of course, the wild rose.

Apple

Paring knife

Sticks, copper rods or tubing (about 36" long) to form pentagram

Shorter rods of equal lengths, depending on what is available or desired

Ball of thick yarn or string

Activities:

Cut the apple 'the other way' and find the star. Check to make sure the batch of apples you buy from shows the star. Some don't pass muster.

String Thing- By skipping 5 spaces repeatedly (5 to 10 to 3 to 8...), after much tossing back and forth around the circle, you will end up with a 12-pointed star. This is an amazing form to behold as it grows. Raise it overhead, lower it to the ground, tilt it, have a child go under it, etc.

Bring-a-Thing- The above-mentioned flowers have five petals. Everything is not perfectly formed within an archetype. A maple leaf is a modification of the star form, for example. So is the hand!

Draw a star within a circle. Look for the pentagon in the middle to be well formed.

Be A Star- One child (Star Child*) stands spread-eagled. A second child (Angel) holds a string above the first's head (H). A third child (Star Weaver) then passes the string successively to left foot (LF), right hand (RH), left hand (LH), right foot (RF, and back to head (H). The order again is: (H), (LF), (RH), (LH), (RF) and (H). Make sure the Star Child holds the string securely on her fingers and that the string is secured underfoot. Demonstrate with one group and then break up into groups of three.   *Other names may be chosen, or none at all.

Daniel makes the pentagonal shape from the inside on the outside by connecting the points of the star. Note that now the pentagon is right side up, whereas on the inside it is upside down.

Make the star with tubing, straws, dowels, etc.

Walk the Star- Children or markers demarcate the five points of the star. Starting at the top, one by one the children walk to all points before returning to the top. They may walk the usual way or move always facing the same direction.

Variation- One child stands at each of the 5 points of the star. Using a rhythm 123, or 1234, etc., they move simultaneously, following the one before them in formation.

The number five points the way to exciting future studies involving the Fibonacci sequence and the Golden Ratio.

SIX

Materials:

Yarn or string.

Craft stick triangles from #3

6-petaled flowers- (Lily family) includes daffodil, hyacinth, crocus, anemone, etc.

Vegetables of 6-fold nature- green pepper, carrot slice

Honeycomb

Amethyst points (from mineral and gem suppliers); well worth the effort

6 stones or balls of similar size; hamburger buns; coins; metal washers, etc.

Hoops

Activities:

Using the already made triangles, create 6-pointed stars (hexagrams).

The String Thing- Form the Beautiful Triangle within the circle. Then take a second ball of yarn and run it from place #6 to #10 to #2. Note that there is a hexagon inside which is regular, or even, when all the small triangles that stick out are the same size.

Run another piece of string between the six points, forming a hexagon on the outside of the star. Draw this.

Doodling- One of the things to be discovered when doodling is the asterisk star formed by drawing lines from the center to each of the angles.

Try moving the hexagon around the meadow, the way the circle was moved with #1. It is helpful to look at the person at the angle opposite you. Spokes on a wheel is a good image. Even if it doesn't succeed, the attempt will have lessons to offer.

Using stones or uniform objects, create a triangle with 3 on the bottom, then 2, then one on the top.

Here is an opportunity for the children to get to experience honey from a honeycomb. Demonstrate how perfectly the cells of the honeycomb fit together.

Bring-a-Thing- Look for hexagonal objects: shower tiles, stop signs, etc., and, of course, the flowers. Green peppers and carrots are vegetables that exhibit six-ness.

Most of the six-petaled flowers belong to the lily family. It is interesting to note that the members of this family usually grow from bulbs whose roots are little more than hairs, while those in the rose family have roots that reach down deep into the earth.

Find the hexagon within the 16-in-1 Beautiful Triangle.

Build a frame around the 6 balls; hexagonal. The fit is perfect

Many intricate flower-like geometrical forms can be constructed using a compass, but this is best left for children in higher grades.

Distribute amethyst points. Make it a special moment. Perhaps show how quartz, amethyst and citrine all embody the hexagonal structure. All three are composed of silica but were heated differently within the earth at the time of their formation.

Especially with #6, one could go on and on making beautiful and interesting connections. However this book, as it related to younger elementary students, is meant to whet the children's appetites and inspire enthusiasm. Restraint is called for in order to leave them a bit hungry. Adults, however, may be inspired to deepen their understanding. This will in time bear fruit for their children as well as for themselves.

The following passage was originally going to be included in the text, however it goes a little far for the younger children. It could be inserted into the text at your discretion when working with older children. It certainly is an engaging construction. I had it situated just before Anne passed out her honeycomb.

Andrew never tired of making the circles taking a bite out of each other with. One day, he found himself adding a third circle.

"What's good with two might be good with three," he said.

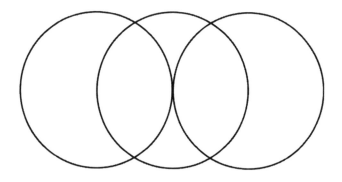

"Look at this, Nick," he called.

Nick looked at it thoughtfully. Then he took a stick and started connecting points. Before long he called out excitedly, "Here it is, the six-sided form, again!"

The children came running.

"How did you do it?" asked Daniel.

"Well, wherever the circles touched, and of course the centers, is where I made the connections," said Nick, feeling like he'd done something special.

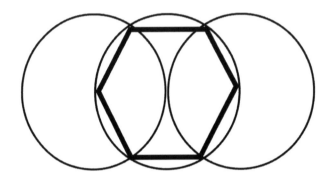

"Amazing!" said Rosemary.

"Incredible,!" said Robin.

"Beautiful!" said Mary.

SEVEN

Materials:

Stained glass in the rainbow colors can be obtained from any stained glass shop. Be sure the edges are ground down, or wrapped with copper foil. Ask how to do this in the glass shop. By the way, they make great Christmas tree ornaments.

Circular and spherical objects of uniform sized marbles, washers, coins of the same denomination; hamburger buns, etc.

7 round stones, the heavier the better

Watercolor paints

Watercolor paper

Activities:

Take the time to enter into the qualities of the colors of the rainbow. Ask what the children experienced of them. Give the image of the color lifting off a lemon, or of a green mist rising from a leaf, etc.

Find the Dippers in the night sky.

Using coins, washers, colored paper circles, marbles, apples, or hamburger buns, arrange the six around a seventh. They will fit perfectly if they are all the same size. Note the star form within.

Trace a circle, and then trace six more around it with each touching the circumference of the inner one and the ones on either side.

Have children say the days of the week backwards. Saying anything backwards is strengthening.

Line up the seven stones and move one stone away, then a second, and so on, imprinting in a bodily way these basic number facts. This particularly helps children having difficulty developing number sense. The experience may be generalized to other number facts, ie.,which combinations of addends make any number..

Bring-a-Thing- Use small bits of colored paper to replace the flower petals in recreating the rainbow.

The String Thing- Mark a circle with 7 equally spaced points. The distance between them is obviously more than with 12 and slightly less than with 6. Skipping every other point will create the seven-star, or heptagon.

Construct the intersecting circles of Sir Twain with a third ring intersecting it from above. Trace it on the sidewalk or playground and hop in each section as in hopscotch. Color each section a different color with chalk. Invent a game.

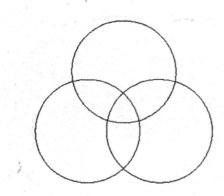

Sing or play the scale, demonstrating how the eighth note is a repeat of the first, the octave.

Paint swatches of the various colors, a rainbow, or a color wheel.

Derive all seven colors from the three primary ones, blue, yellow and red.

Display the seven pieces of colored glass on your nature table, or on the windowsill. DON'T LET THE CHILDREN HOLD THEM NEAR THEIR EYES unless they are supervised.

Alternatively, fill bottles with water colored with food dye in the rainbow colors.

Flowers don't tend to have seven-foldness. Clematis and the heads of poppy seed pods are two that do.

EIGHT

Materials:

Craft stick squares from #4

2 large square pieces of construction paper

3" square Post- it Notes

3/16" wooden dowels, 2, 3 or 4 ft. long

Thin cardboard strips about ¾"X 4" to write OTTO

Large square of paper or cardboard

Chess board; chess pieces

Materials to model your own chess pieces with : beeswax, clay, etc. (optional)

Activities

Although there is no scene relating directly to this in Sarah's story, we can hearken back to *King Maximo and the Number Knights.* There, Sir Otto finds that, by engraving his name on a metal bracelet, and bending the two ends to meet each other, the numeral 8 is formed. This, too, is the figure 8, or the sign for infinity, which children are so fond of. In any case, making this adds a bit to the wonder of numbers. This can be done nicely on a strip of cardboard, using colored pencil.

Breaking the Branch- If possible, give the children a chance to break a stick into pieces as Sir Otto did. This is a great experience, anticipating the study of fractions in the following years. It is well worth the investment. The bodily experience achieves something that serves the later "head work". There is no need to speak of fractions. Simply do it. Referring to halves or quarters in passing is sufficient up to the third grade.

Get an easy to snap wooden dowel about 3/16" thick and 2 to 4 ft. in length. First, using a yardstick, measure 8 equal segments. 24", 36" and 48" are divisible by eight. 24" divides into 8 segments 3" long; 36" divides up into 8 segments 4 1/2" long, while 48" divides into 6" long segments. Score the dowel with a saw, nail clippers, or pliers to get a clean break. When snapping the stick, place fingers on either side near the score marks. Later, what you've done may be shown on a yardstick.

Make an octagon with the stick segments. Make one square and then lay the other four sticks on top, turned 90 degrees. The protruding triangles should be the same size. Center them over the middle of the sides of the first square.

Make an octagon with Post-it Notes- Rotate one square one half turn over the other so that 4 equal triangles stick out. Fold over or snip off the triangles to arrive at the octagon. This may be done as a warm-up, before attempting to make the octagon with sticks (above). In some circumstances this may suffice to give the experience of the octagon.

Constructing the castle floor plan using Post-it Notes- First make the main octagon, using the two square Post-it Notes. Then cut another square into 4, and then each of these into 4 again. This gives 16 squares with which to construct the 8 towers. Small strips of Post-it Notes may connect the corners to form the walls.

The String Thing- Making an octagon in the circle or on the board requires some ingenuity. For the first square the string jumps from the top to 3 to 6 to 9 and on to 12. The second square, however, requires that children or peg dolls are placed outside their accustomed positions If using peg dolls children must hold the dolls in positions 1 ½, 4 1/2, 7 ½ and 10 ½, 3 spaces apart.

Bring-a-Thing- Octagonal forms in nature are not as commonly found as pentagonal or hexagonal ones. Flowers with 8-foldness include: Celandine, Cosmos, Passionflower, and Gazania. .

The chessboard/checkerboard holds many lessons to be discovered.

Scene with Hugh and Nick: Follow their directions, dividing the paper to get the 64 squares of the chessboard. Perhaps do freehand first and then use a ruler or straightedge.

Freehand drawing of octagon- Continue sketching squares preparatory to drawing the octagon. You may find that freehand drawing of the octagon is more of a challenge than younger children can handle. Try using sticks to form the angle's opening.

From Square to Octagon- Start with a square Post-it note. Cut away each corner to arrive at an octagon. Make sure that the triangles you cut off have two legs of equal length. All four triangles should be the same size; all eight sides should be the same length.

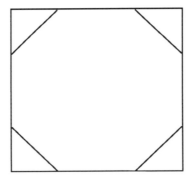

NINE

Materials:

Hazel nuts, acorns, glass beads, etc., or counters of various sorts.

Tic-Tac-Toe form

Craft sticks (3 triangles from earlier work may be reused)

Cardboard and crayons

Activities:

Magic Square- Make a magic square out of cardboard with gilded or multicolored numbers. Even better, glue the cardboard to a 1" thick block of wood of the same dimensions. The pattern is as follows:

8 1 6

3 5 7

4 9 2

Remember, the three numbers add up to 15 in every direction. You might change the story and not give out the clue that 15 is the sum of the three addends, as Sarah did.

Draw the magic square in the dirt or on asphalt using chalk.

Perhaps one of the characters recites while figuring: 8 and 1 are 9, and 6 more makes 15, etc. This is beneficial for many children <u>who</u> have trouble adding.

For older children you may introduce the 4X4 magic square with 16 spaces.

Square Numbers--Learn by heart: 1 4 9 16 25 36 49 64 81 100 121 144. Or, 1X1 is 1; 2X2 is 4; 3X3 is 9; 4X4 is 16, and so on. This need not be tied to multiplication, <u>per se</u>, just rote memorization like learning a verse. Mastery is achieved by reciting this series without pausing, a good challenge. Just begin with the first four, and gradually add another and another. 2<u>5</u> & 3<u>6</u> (5 fives and 6 sixes. Helps build familiarity with and sense of wonder about the times tables.

Enneagram- Rotate three triangles upon themselves until you arrive at a 9-pointed star (enneagram).

The 9-pointed star (enneagram) can be drawn in 3 ways, after having marked off the circle with 9 points:

1) Connect every other point; 2) Connect every third point;3) Connect every fourth point.

To go from the square of nine to the X requires moving four stones, the middle one on each side.

This triangle is a good seqway to ten, if you imagine a tenth ball in the middle.

TEN

Materials:

Clay; (I recommend Sargent Art's non-hardening modeling clay)

Cardboard, tree bark, picture matting scraps, or other stiff material for shields

Thin dowels, disposable chopsticks, shish kabob skewers (with points clipped off)

Activities

Roman soldiers- Use 10 pieces of clay in a size that is convenient. Vary the heights of the soldiers if desired. Cut 10 small, rectangular pieces of cardboard for shields and number them I-X. Embed them in the clay by gently folding the "arms" over the shield. Next, press the stick (spear) into the side of the clay. Add the heads, giving them individual characteristics, or not. Aluminum foil might be used to create a helmet. You could even make a plume.

Roman Numerals- A brief study of Roman numerals is worth the effort. After all, the Super Bowls are enumerated that way. To add Roman numerals is to break down all numbers into (V)s, (X)s and (I)s. Of course (I)s to the right of a number V or X make it one larger (V+I= VI), or six; (X+I=XI), or eleven. When placed to the left of a V or X, they are one less. A simple way of adding is to deconstruct the numerals and add up the 3 columns.

Thus, VII plus IV plus XIII plus XVII, or 7+4+13+17 would look like this:

V II

I V

 X III

 X

 <u>V II</u>

-1 +35 +7 =41

There are descriptions of multiplication using Roman Numerals, but this can be a cumbersome process. Perhaps you will see why Sir Ten gave way to Sir Double Digit.

Bring-a-Thing- An encounter with a meter stick provides a glimpse of the metric system.

10-Pointed Star (Decagram)- Construction of the Decagram star is quite similar to that for the Enneagram star. First mark off the circle with 10 points. Then connect every other point, every third point, or every fourth point.

ELEVEN

Materials:

5' long piece of ½"X2" pine board baseboard moulding

or

Small-sized Hershey bars 2 ½" X ¼" (most commonly found around Halloween)

Gold paint- Modern Masters Metallic Paint Collection; or gold foil

Back saw and miter box (for cutting moulding); or it could be cut at the lumberyard

Small blackboard or slate; and chalk

Activities:

Recreate the number 11 found on Sir Doubledigit's coat of arms. Stand the single bar to the right of the stack of 10 bars. This establishes a concrete image for number 11, the first number that clearly demonstrates 'place value'.

Cut the 5 ft. long piece of wood into eleven pieces 5 in. long. There will just be a tad left over. Each bar's length will be the same as the height of the 10 bars stacked up. This, in itself, is a good activity for children to watch.

Paint the bars gold, or wrap them in gold foil.

You can make the gold bars nearly any size. It is only necessary that the length of a single bar be as long as the combined height of the other 10 stacked bars.

Perfect random synchronicity occurs when using small-sized Hershey bars (2 ½" X ¼)." If you stack 10 of them, they stand exactly as high as the length of the single candy bar.

Set up stack of gold bars, and place some loose ones beside it on a table recreating the '27' scene from *King Maximo and the Number Knights.*

Have a slate or a picture of a slate on the board.

Place value- Ask, *"when is 2 greater than 7?"* Recreate the illustration from King Maximo, showing ones and tens. This provides a segway into the study of "place value" which will stay with the children. Give other problems involving face value.

TWELVE

Materials:

Clay bars; (I recommend Sargent Art's non-hardening modeling clay)

13 magnetized steel balls (optional)

4 popsicle stick triangles

3 popsicle stick squares

 Ball of thick yarn or string.

Activities:

Discuss what it is like to see things from another perspective. Picture a rock or a tree through different seasons and weather conditions. How is it experienced by different animals? How do different people view it? Is it for its beauty, practical uses, etc.

String Thing- You may repeat the activity found in the chapter on #5. Pass the ball of yarn around the circle to every fifth place starting at 0/12. (5,10,3,8,1,6,11,4,9,2,7,12). It will end with 12-pointed star. This helps demonstrate, in summation, how numbers are interrelated.

Twelve is a good lead into the times tables, multiplication, division, and factoring. Twelve is, in a real sense, the "King of Numbers." Show how it can be divided by more numbers than any other number. Its factors are 1,2,3,4,6 and 12.

Using two overlapping hexagons make the 12-pointed star, or dodecagon, as it is called.

Make it also using 4 triangles or 3 squares.

Bring-a-Thing-   Egg carton; ruler; a dozen donuts; 12 stones

Make clear that the pentagon is essential to the structure of the dodecahedron. This is one final demonstration of the interrelation of numbers to one another.

To make the magical figure (cuboctahedron), either with magnetic marbles or with clay, arrange 6 balls around a central ball. Then add a triangle of 3 balls on either side. First let children try to discover this on their own.

Cutting the clay into 13 equal parts will assure that all the balls will be the same size. 1" diameter is a practicable size. It is beneficial to take any opportunity to experience fractions in practical, hands-on situations, before formally teaching fractions in a more abstract way.

The writing of this book was undertaken primarily to demonstrate and underscore the importance and efficacy of teaching what is otherwise academic content through story, movement and art.--- H. S.

Songs of Joccomo

Composed in pentatonic mode

1

(G) (G) (G) (B)

One is the sun

(A) (B) (A) (G)

One is the sky

(G) (G) (G) (B)

One is the world

(B) (AB) (A)(G)

And one am I

2

(D) (B) (A) (B)

Two are my eyes

(B) (DB) (A) (B)

Ears hands and feet

(D) (D) (B)

Dark and light

(B) (AGA) (B)

At sunset meet

3

  (E)   (B)   (A)   (B)

STONES PLANTS AND BEASTS

  (G)   (D) (A) (E)

EARTH AIR AND SEA

  (G)   (A) (B)   (A)   (G)   (E)

WITH MY HEAD HEART AND HANDS

  (G)   (B)   (A) (G) (B)

THE WORLD DO I MEET

4

  (E) (E) (E)   (B)

TABLES AND CHAIRS

   (B)   (E)   (E) (B)

SHOUTS STOUT FOURSQUARE

  (B)   (B)   (A) (G)   (A)   (B)

FLOORS AND CEILINGS AND WALLS

  (B)   (E)   (E) (B) (B) (E)   (E)   (B)

FOUR LIMBS TO LABOR ON THE EARTH

  (B) (A)   (G)   (E) (G)   (A) (B)

WINTER SPRING SUMMER AND FALL

5

(D)   (B) (G)

FIVE FINGERS

(D)   (B)(G)

FIVE TOES

(G)   (A) (A)   (A)   (D)   (B)(G)

FIVE PETALS HAS THE ROSE

(D)   (B)   (G)   (D)   (B)(G)

FIVE RAYS HAS THE STAR

(G)   (A)(D)

SO NEAR

(D)   (G)

SO FAR

6

(B) (D)   (B)   (A) (G)   (A) (B)   (D) (B) (A)

SIX SIDES HAVE THE CELLS OF THE HONEYCOMB

(G)   (B)   (A)(G) (A)   (B) (D)

THAT FIT TOGETHER SO WELL

(B)   (D)   (B)   (A) (G)(A)   (B) (A)   (E)

SIX WALLS DO AMETHYST CRYSTALS SHOW

(E)   (G)(E)   (G)   (G) (A)(G) (A)   (B)(G)(E)

SIX PETALS HAVE THE LILY AND DAFFODIL

(E) (G)   (E)   (G)   (A)   (G)   (A)   (B)

IN EACH FLAKE OF SNOW THAT COMES DOWN

(E) (G) (E) (G)   (A) (G)   (A) (B)

A DIFFERENT SIXNESS IS FOUND

7

G)(A)　(B)　(D)　(E)　(D)　(B)　(D)

SEVEN IS SEEN IN THE RAINBOW

(D)　(E)　(D) (B) (A)(G)

THE STARS IN THE DIPPER

(A)　(D)　(B) (A)　(B)

THE DAYS OF THE WEEK

(E)(G) (A)　(B) (A)　(G)

SEVEN IS COUNTED AS

(D) (D)　(B)

SIX PLUS ONE

(A)　(G)　(A)

FIVE PLUS TWO

(B)(A) (G)　(D)

FOUR PLUS 3

8

(D)   (B)   (A)   (G)

TWO TWOS ARE FOUR

(E)   (G)   (A)   (B)

TWO FOURS ARE EIGHT

(B)   (D)   (B) (A)   (G)(G)

WHAT COULD BE MORE EVEN

(G)   (E)   (G) (A)   (B)

THAN OUR NUMBER EIGHT

9

(A) (A)   (E)

NUMBER NINE

(D)   (B)   (A)   (B)

THREE ROWS OF THREE

(A) (G) (G)   (B)

A PERFECT SQUARE

(A) (A) (G)

DO I SEE

10

(G)   (E)   (G) (A)

TEN LOVES TO COUNT

(B)   (A)   (G)(A)

COME LET'S SEE

(G)   (A)(A)   (B)(B)

TEN TWENTY THIRTY

(A)(A)   (D)(B)

FORTY   FIFTY

11

(G)(G)(G)   (B)   (A) (B)   (A) (G)

ELEVEN LEADS THE WAY TO SHOW

(G)   (G)(G)(G)   (G)   (B)

THAT NUMERALS ARE PLACED

(B)   (A)(B)   (A)   (G)

WHERE THEY SHOULD GO

12

(D)   (B)   (A)   (G) (A)

TWELVE IS THE NUMBER

(B)   (A)   (G)   (E)   (D)

THAT CHARTS SPACE AND TIME

(G)   (A) (A)   (A)   (G)   (A)

TWELVE INCHES MAKES ONE FOOT

(A)   (A)   (E)   (G)   (E)

TWELVE MONTHS THE YEAR'S SIGNS

(G)   (A) (G)   (G) (A)

TWELVE HOURS OF DAY

(B)   (A) (G)   (E)   (E)

TWELVE HOURS OF NIGHT

(B)   (A)   (G)   (A)   (D)

WHEN WE THINK OF TWELVE

(D) (D)   (B)   (A) (B)   (D)

ALL THE WORLD IS MADE RIGHT

Made in the USA
Monee, IL
04 May 2021